MEN
IN
WHITE
APPAREL

BY

ANN REE COLTON

ARC PUBLISHING COMPANY
P.O. BOX 1138
GLENDALE, CALIFORNIA 91209

Third Printing

Printed in the United States of America
DeVorss & Co., P.O. Box 550, Marina del Rey, CA 90291

Lovingly Dedicated

to

Jonathan
and
Jethro

FOREWORD

Each person has a Dark or Death Angel. From the moment of birth, the Dark Angel holds the scales of balance between life and death. The Dark Angel, working with the destroying principle, enables the cells of the body to die. The Dark Angel also enables one to erase or forget memories which sear and pain.

When the time has come for one to die, his name is called by the Dark Angel. If one is fearful of death, and refuses to respond to the first and second calls of the Dark Angel, he must yield to the third and final call.

When one has responded to the mechanics of dying without fear in previous lives, he sees the Dark Angel as bright and luminous during the last moments of dying, and after death. If one believes in eternal life, he beholds the Dark Angel as the Bright Angel of Resurrection.

CONTENTS

First Heaven		
Saviours and Prophets	△ △ △ △ △	
Saints	△ △ △ △ △	
	(Cloisters of Heaven)	
Presences of Heaven and the Risen Dead	△ △ △ △ △	
Lighted Corridors of the Risen Dead	△ △ △ △ △	
Pavilions of Light. The Quickened Dead ready for rebirth.	(Halls of Learning) △ △ △ △ △	
Paradise		
The Purgatorial Caverns where instruction is given.	▽ ▽ ▽ ▽ ▽	
World-subconscious. Purgatorial anesthesia. Purgatorial tumults.		
Well-meaning earthbound. Evil earthbound.	□ □ □ □ □ □ □ □ □ ■ ■ ■ ■ ■ ■ ■ ■ ■	

Hall of Records

1.

DEATH AND THE SOUL

O man, run thy race, and take thy rest when thy race is run. Learn that death, the quiet time of thy soul, is a healing time; for the wondrous way of God hath prepared for thee a place beyond time and haste. Let thy tempestuous will be still. Put aside thy playthings and thy graven idols. Behold the jewel in which thou art encased; for the light of the soul is thine own eternal home.

All things of God are of grandeur interwoven with simplicity. The souls of men are geared to birth, life, sleep, and death. The life of each man contains a record of struggle, effort, power, glory. Not one particle of action, thought, or emotion is lost within God's Eternal Plan.

Death, seemingly so far from life, is ever-present within life. Men with greater dimen-

1

sions of soul look upon death as an inevitable act in the drama of life; they play their parts in the drama of the living and of the dead with equal acumen, integrity, peace, and joy. Such men reassure the doubtful, the fearful.

As one grows, matures, and evolves, he no longer sees death as an opponent or as an adversary; he sees death as an inalterable necessity. Such understanding provides the soul with the power to unite the good works of this life with the essences of heaven.

The average person knows very little about his true identity. Enmeshed in a world of competition, force, and pressure, and often lacking creativity, he fails during the complete lifetime to communicate with himself. Death compels each one to communicate with himself—to lay open and to expose the motives and the actions experienced in the life just lived. All persons enter into some form of self-communication after death.

Regardless of agnostic theories, atheistic disbeliefs, or religious training, in all persons there is an immortal memory of life eternal.

The body of man—his cells and his frame—dies; but that which imaged him, formed him, and gave him life cannot die. The true identity of man, being a projection of God, is deathless.

Death is a soul-experience. To gain the greater soul-experience in death, one must die not only to the physical body; he also must die to his theoretical or theological beliefs concerning the life after death. When the one who dies limits himself to doctrinal religious beliefs, atheistic beliefs, or materialistic beliefs, he interferes with the soul's experience in death.

The atheist believes that the physical and sensual life is the totality of expression. The cynic believes that men have created a heaven through the imagination. The materialist believes that if one is good in the physical world, and if there *is* a heaven, the good that he has done will earn for him a rightful place in heaven. The traditional religious mind believes that man survives death and remains perpetually either in a state of darkness due to his evil works, or in a state of light if he has been the doer of good works. The spiritist believes that the dead continue their physical world interests and actions while living in heaven. The metaphysical mind rules out the belief of hell and believes in the afterlife as heaven. The spiritual mind believes in the survival and continuation of consciousness after death, and in a progressive state of instruction after death in varied degrees of purgatory and heaven. The spiritual mind knows that men are reborn repeatedly to the earth, and that each life is an opportunity to grow, to develop, and to evolve. One with a spiritual mind also believes that the duration or length of each life is determined by the soul and the need for expression.

Death is a covenant with the soul. Before one dies, he makes a covenant with the soul to die in the way he will die. The Guardian Angel, working with the soul, conditions and prepares one for death, regardless of what kind of death is experienced. If there be death by accident, war, violence, or natural cause, the mercy of God enables each person to intuit, inwardly, the ending of the physical life.

Thus, death comes not to anyone out of timing.

The equilibrium of existence is a mighty balancer in the life of each person. Therefore, when men say, "It is the Will of God", after someone has died, this statement comes not from surface beliefs, but from a wellspring of intuition fed and nourished by the immortal attributes of the soul.

The atheistic mind, on seeing death by violence, cynically reconfirms his disbelief in a God of Love who permits His children to die by violence or pain. One who discerns the true meaning of death intuits and accepts God's law of equation and justice. It is believed by those with spiritual insight that death through violence is caused by former-life aggressive tendencies and irreverence for the individuality of others.

> *Then said Jesus unto him, Put up again thy sword into his place: for all they that take the sword shall perish with the sword.*
> —St. Matthew 26:52

During a violent death, fear carries a powerful antidote; for the Guardian Angel and the Angel of Death place upon a person subjected to a violent death the death anesthesia, which anesthetizes the fear. Shock immediately preceding death increases the velocity of the soul's action, and the entry into the world of the dead is one of startling clarity. Everything in the new world is magnified far beyond that which is experienced in natural death.

When one dies by what is called an "accident", he has failed in some manner to observe the law of timing in this life and in previous lives. When one dies a natural death, or through natural causes, he has earned in former lives the grace of years and longevity, so that he might mellow and mature to the period and the civilization in which he lives.

When masses of people die through cataclysms, earthquakes, the elements, drownings, genocide, or war, these persons are recalled from life by their souls. They relinquish their claim on life so that they might prepare themselves in the inner worlds for future lives on earth whereby they may have a better expression in a higher form of civilization.

THE DEATH WISH

When a person has incurred heavy debts in previous lives, he may experience in the present life a prolonged death wish, or desire to die. This sometimes attracts to the person a serious illness, bordering on death. The sickness is, in reality, an act of grace enabling the person to bring to balance the debts of the past lives while remaining in the physical world. From this time forth, he no longer has the death wish; for in the crisis of his illness he has intuited, inwardly, the cause of the death wish, and he has made agreement with his soul to remain in the world and fulfill that which his soul asks of him.

There exists a more dangerous death wish —the death wish accompanied by an obsession to take one's own life. This death wish induces the thought of suicide into the mind of a person who is heavily laden with seemingly irremediable debts of former lives. Since life appears to be useless, purposeless, and at a dead-end, the person sees no other way than to end his existence. Such compulsions, when overwhelming, are consummated in the taking of one's own life. Therefore, rather than resolving his debts, he adds to the debts by committing one of the greatest of all offences —the sin against the Holy Ghost.

Persons who end their lives by their own hands are caught and suspended, after death, between the world of the living and the world of the dead. Having failed to finish their physical compulsions, they literally haunt former environments. One who takes his life remains in this suspended state for the length of time that he would have lived had he remained in the physical body.

The after-death suspension of a suicide is more painful than the ordinary earthbound state; for a person who has committed suicide cannot enter into the rhythmic formulas of purgatory in the same manner as one who has died from other causes.

GRIEF FOR THE DEAD

No one is ever the same after having grieved for the dead. Grief is a powerful catalyst, changing the perspective, illuminating the mind, and making more sensitive the hardened places within the heart. To one of a materialistic nature, the loss by death is a harsh and disciplinary experience. To one who has unclarified faith, grieving for the dead is a somber and maturing experience. To one who has spiritual awareness, loss by death is an experience of initiation and revelation.

Grief has the power to change and to transform a selfish nature into a more magnanimous temperament. Grief has the power to give insight, and to extend the buds of sympathy. Grief also has the power to draw men closer to heaven and to the reality of heaven. During intense grief, the soul expands one's thoughts as to the meaning of life and death, heaven and earth.

Grief has the power to cleanse away the materiality and cynicism in the thoughts of a person. It also has the power to free one from his fear of death. If one gains a spiritual experience through grief, in the future his world will be colored with immortal thoughts and actions.

Where there is grief for the dead, and a

feeling of sincere bereavement, something of
grace is given to the living, through which
their grief may extend their knowledge of
things of the soul. After the loss of a loved
one, many persons begin to delve into the
reason why one must die, and they also wish
to know if there is a life after death. From
that time onward, their lives are more spiritually inclined.

Every day men die. Some are grieved for
with genuine grief. The death of those who
have been incumbrances is sometimes looked
upon as a relief. Men die in prison, in dis-
grace. Men die as paupers, or impoverished.
Men, who have purchased the affection of
those around them, die in cold palaces. The
world is indifferent to their dying. There is
a burden upon the souls of those who leave
not grief in the world. When grief is genuine
and sincere, the angels and their ministering
helps touch the grieving, and the Angels of
Death find their task easier.

Grief has many stages: poignant, deep,
anguished, nostalgic, reverent, and grateful
reminiscence. When grief has moved to the

stage of grateful reminiscence, the tie between the one grieving and the one dead has been resolved; and the memory of the one dead lives in the reverent thoughts of that one in the world who loved him.

Persons harm themselves when they are bitter or unjust toward the dead. Hate is like solder, uniting one with the dead rather than separating him from the dead. Hate after death wreaks havoc upon the living and delays the rise of the one who has died.

The materialistic person is never prepared for the death of one close to him. The death of someone valuable to him comes as a shock; and, in some instances, he feels death to be an intrusion and a personal affront. Death, in its finality, is appalling to the materialistic and cynical mind. Rather than softening such a person's hardened outlook, death accentuates it; and, in this crucial time of loss, the materialistic person, failing to have reverence for death, looks upon the loss of one close to him as an inconvenience.

When a person bitterly resents the natural consequence of separation through death, and turns his face away from the greatest of all griefs—the loss by death, he is denying the sacred theme of life. The shadow of his bitterness falls between him and the one who has died.

After the death of a person important to them, those who are heavily sensual are given the opportunity, through grief, to become less sensual. If there be no genuine grief, the sensuous person falls deeper into sensuality and cynicism, and fails to understand death's meaning.

When one grieves blindly and egotistically, he is concerned solely with his own loss, and does not consider the one who has died, or his whereabouts. By thinking only of the absence of the physical presence of the one who complemented him, and made him more comfortable in his needs and desires, he closes the door to the meaning of death.

The most selfish of persons, on being faced with grief for the dead, is exposed for a brief time, though unwillingly, to the greater truths supporting the reality of eternal life.

DEATH OF THE YOUNG

Of all deaths which occur, the death of an infant or a child is the least understood. "Why does God permit a child to die? Why should a child, the very essence of innocence and purity, be taken from the world? Did the parents fail, that the child should be taken from them?" These questions have been an enigma to those who love children and who cherish them. It is commonly believed by persons in formal religions that the death of a child is the Will of God, and that the child is being protected from the evils of the world. This belief limits that which God is seeking to say through the meaning of death.

When parents have little or no knowledge of life after death or of the continuity of lives, they suffer a tragic hopelessness in the loss of their young. If parents are emotionally immature, the death of a child inflicts a heavy stigmata, and their thwarted love of the child leaves lasting wounds, often colored by a sense of guilt, or a feeling of unworthiness. When parents are spiritually inclined, they know that each one is immortal, and that all associations are part of the Plan of God. In the event of the loss of an infant or child, such parents understand that a vital and necessary association between their souls and the soul of the child has been fulfilled.

Parents who have reverently given birth to a child look upon the gift of life as a sacred trust. When there is loss of their child by death, reverent parents are drawn closer to an understanding of the purpose of death. During the time of their greatest grief, they are strengthened by the presences of heaven. Such parents do not search for their shortcomings in the loss of a child. They look upon the visitation of the child as a blessing, in which a greater love lived in their home for a few hours, days, or years; they know, in their hearts, that such love was an immortal touch of grace, and can never die.

> *Take heed that ye despise not one of these little ones; for I say unto you, That in heaven their angels do always behold the face of my Father which is in heaven.*
>
> —St. Matthew 18:10

Children who die before the seventh year are awakc to their angels instantly after death. It is within the power of these children to give comfort and solace to their parents and to assuage their grief. Such parents invariably pray to replace the child just lost; for the child's love from heaven inspires the parents to give birth to another child. In rare instances, the same child may be reborn to the parents. This would occur only through some act of grace earned in former lives by the sorrowing parents.

The pain, grief, and suffering a mother and father experience in the loss of an infant or child increase their capacity to love one another and to cherish all loved ones. The presences of heaven, inclusive of the angels, work unceasingly to give comfort to those who grieve through death. The Men in White Apparel and the Guardian Angels of the dead come close to a sorrowing mother or father, so that those who grieve might be comforted.

MEN IN WHITE APPAREL

The Men in White Apparel, a part of the

heavenly company called the Elect, have never lived in the physical world; they are spiritual beings who watch over, instruct, and shepherd the dead. Their work is directed toward the giving of solace and instruction to the dead, and comfort to those grieving for the dead.

The Angels of Death and the Men in White Apparel are as the right arm of Jesus working with the dead. These heavenly beings minister to the dead, enabling the dead to cross the abyss between earth and heaven.

The Men in White Apparel are sometimes seen by those who grieve for the dead. In the ascension of Jesus, the Men in White Apparel stood by to reconcile the disciples to the ascension of Jesus.

And when he had spoken these things, while they beheld, he was taken up; and a cloud received him out of their sight.

And while they looked stedfastly toward heaven as he went up, behold, two men stood by them in white apparel;

Which also said, Ye men of Galilee, why stand ye gazing up into heaven? this same Jesus,

*which is taken up from you into heaven, shall
so come in like manner as ye have seen him
go into heaven.*

—Acts 1:9-11

2.

PREPARATION FOR DEATH

And now thy soul saith, "Thou hast ripened".
Let the winter of thy years place the cloak of
remembrance about thee. Thou standest now
between life and death; and thy soul is the
chooser of the way. Look thou not back with
regret, neither look thou forward with fear.
Learn what thou didst desire; and look back
upon what thou didst do with charity, with wis-
dom. Let the decaying season remind thee that
the falling leaf will nourish the coming bud of
the spring. Welcome what is said to thee of dy-
ing, and of the life to come.

In the life of each person, there are four
stages of adjustment to death: (1) the be-
wildering time when the child learns that
there is an end to life; (2) when one suffers
grief after losing someone close to him by
death; (3) when a person is faced with ill-

nesses or crises which could be the cause of his own death; and (4) the pre-purgatory stage, or preparation for death, which begins in the 63rd year.

A child is prepared to understand death's meaning when he sees his first pet die. Children, being so close to heaven until the seventh year, need only a small reminder to be reassured of the greater truths in death and life. If a child has the grace to have loving and reverent parents, the explanation of death will be absorbed into his naive emotions and thoughts. Though grieving over the loss of his beloved pet, he will accept death as part of life and change. Should a parent, through his own lack of an understanding of death, bruise the child in this time by refusing to speak of death's meaning in its proper sense, death becomes an awesome and fearful thing to the child; this feeling persists throughout his life. Thus, the parent has planted the first seeds of insecurity relating to the child's affection for places, objects, and persons in his life.

Each time one grieves for the dying or the

dead, he is more fully prepared for his own death. The sorrows suffered when wars bring death and desolation remind men that death has many faces. These sorrows prepare those who are philosophically inclined to comprehend the inevitableness of death, and to confirm their belief that dying and living are the sowing and reaping of a Mighty Hand directing the destinies of all men.

Persons who suffer lingering illnesses are close to their Death Angels at all times. Each serious illness is a preparation for death. Sicknesses loosen the rigidity of the personality, and prepare men to accept death with naturalness and peace.

To those who reach their mature years, death is as a bell which begins its tolling in the 63rd year. With the ensuing years, its sound grows increasingly louder, shutting out the sounds of the world. All persons who reach the 63rd year begin to hear, more and more, the summoning of the sound calling them to a greater life beyond the life in the world.

When one meets death before the 63rd year,

there are other ways in which he is prepared to make the adjustment to death. His Guardian Angel induces upon him a sixth-sense apprehension, preparing him for death. Through certain symbols in dreams and also in his deeper thoughts, he is prepared, inwardly, for the approaching death.

In the 63rd year, one begins to receive instruction from his Death Angel. He enters into a unique dream state at night. He dreams of childhood environments and associations, of parents and grandparents. In his dreams, he recapitulates his childhood beliefs and wonders. In the daytime, he comes closer to those who age along with him. As one begins the final phase of maturity, and preparation for death, friendships take on more meaning. He is aware, with time being more precious, that each thing has a deeper significance.

When one enters into the pre-purgatorial or death preparation experience with a well-proportioned philosophy (gathered from ethical living in his former years), this period of life can be the crown of life. There is a poetic, nostalgic melancholy accompanying preparation for death. He who has loved life, and has lived life for the love of life, shall meet his death preparation with dignity, humor, wisdom, beauty. Counsel from those near their Death Angel is often farseeing and prophetic. For those who will hear, the wisdom of one ripe in years may be a golden providence.

When death comes naturally, gently, one of advancing years may unite his thoughts with the Recording Angels and, thus, pass on to his descendants the outstanding events experienced in the blood line. He recollects the familiar incidents of the past, and he imprints upon the minds of the young the importance of the ancestral theme. Long before men learned the art of recording the historical cultures in the world, the ancestral memory kept alive the momentous deeds in the blood line.

After the 63rd year, when one desires to travel and to see new places, he is freeing himself from worldly claims and possessions; he is preparing for that largesse of the soul, or the inner knowing that all things belong to

God. Such persons arise with more freedom
in the higher worlds after death.

Until a person reaches the 63rd year, his
conscience is his accuser, weigher, and judge.
After the 63rd year, each person has, in some
degree, a rapport with his soul which magnifies conscience, memory, and motive. When
one thinks of death as a natural condition, the
blessed introspection and retrospection experienced in the latter years brings into the
thoughts and the heart an understanding of
the purpose for which one was born, and prepares him for the state of death.

The pre-purgatory state is mercifully given
of God so that one might temper the harsh
offences of former years, and, thereby, soften
the impact of the adjustment to the purgatorial purification after death. Thus, the one approaching death is offered a perspective of
unusual clarity, and a philosophical vision
into dimensions beyond the self-interest and
competition of the more physically vital years.

Many persons who care for the aged or for
those approaching the dying state comment
upon the fact that the one approaching death

lives continually in the past, speaking of the long-ago events as if they were of the present time. While this is often thought to be a senile condition, it is God's way of preparing man to meet the more somber, after-death purgatorial experience.

The word "purgatorial", meaning to purge out, is in no manner connected with the words "hell" or "punishment" as generally believed. The purgatorial experience before and after death is, in reality, God's equation weighing the purpose and intent within the works of the person—as motivated by his heart, his will, and his mind.

Those who have achieved a balanced maturing, having blended their senses with the seasons throughout life—that is, having lived each portion of life in right timing—intuit the true nature of death, and are well content to spend their latter years and days in a semi-contemplative and receptive state. These maturing persons are inspiring to the young, and give a leavening to the meaning of life; for something courageous and fortifying emanates from their wholesome acceptance of death.

Persons who have resisted life—refusing to accept the ordinary changes in even the most commonplace events, and expecting the intimate persons in their lives to remain the same —look upon death as the enemy. They fail to hear what the Angels of Death would say to them. The years after the 63rd year are years of inner dread, suffering, and fear for one who has failed to listen inwardly to the repeated signals reminding him of the inevitable transitions in life.

Those who suffer the acidity of selfishness in their earlier years become senile in their latter years. These aging ones become a detriment and a terror in the family environment. He who has a bitter, regretful old age grasps rather than holds to the physical reassurances in the world. If one has lived a selfish and possessive life, he is more likely to be obsessed as to physical possessions, such as furniture and heirlooms.

In all men there is the necessity to expurgate their errors and to relieve their consciences. A person, in certain layers of his being, may shut away his conscience, but no matter how brutal he may be, he is never entirely free from his conscience. In the ancient times, to relieve their consciences, men sought the mediative counsel of the elders in their tribes. As men progressed through the ages, they sought the blessing of the prophets of their times, whereby they might absolve their wrong acts. In the age now ending, some persons try to cleanse their consciences by confessing to priests; those who are scientifically inclined take their consciences to psychiatrists.

When men come to understand the soul's action in their lives, they learn that the only true and pure confessional is prayer to God; and that sacred and reverent prayer is the most rewarding manner in which one may alleviate his conscience. Prayer is a confessional, a petition, an act of faith, and a surrender of the will to the Will of God—the Giver of life.

Death is more difficult for those who have not prayed in their lives. Through the continued practice of prayer, one prepares himself for death and for the life after death.

When one prays with a contrite heart throughout life, he lessens the purgatorial action after death. His prayers become the stairs upon which he makes the ascent to heaven.

3.

THE SOUL AND
THE MUSIC OF HEAVEN

Death is a life between existences. Each time one enters the state of death, he moves beyond the horizon of the physical state into a state of conscience and consciousness magnified by the soul. As each one moves over the horizon of death into life after death, the soul says to him: "And what now dost thou bring, O journeying one? What hast thou done? And what dost thou bring from the physical world? Let us sort out the treasures from the trifles. And let us enter into a state of rejoicing for the good done. And let us discard the trifles thou hast gathered along the way."

Poets, from the beginning of the ages, have known of an inner music existing in the world. The forests, the rivers, the streams, the birds, and the sun have sung their songs to the inner ear of the poet. When one dies, the inner ear

is opened in greater or lesser degree. The
music of God's Rule and Law is heard by the
unruly. The music of the angels is placed, un-
sparingly and bountifully, into the ear of the
good. And the music of God's majesty falls
upon the ear of the faithful with a peace
unction, anointing and healing.

Music is used by the soul to assist in the
various stages and steps enacted in death.
Music is the background coordinator during
transition—that is, during the release from
the physical body and birth to the inner
worlds. All who die are accompanied by the
angels and by some form of music; for music
relieves the last tensions of the dead.

At the first moment of death, the Recording
Angel comes close to the one who has died
and places upon him streams of light. The
light is received by the one dead as sound,
music, or tone. If the one dead has lived an
evil life, he receives the light as discordant
and somber sound. This sound is used to
wrench him from the world. If one has lived
a life of goodness and mercy, he receives an

immediate relating to the angelic choirs; the music soothes away his fear of death.

To the pure in heart, joy, rhapsody and ecstasy are part of the death experience. If one has lived a chaste life beyond the reproach of his Guardian Angel, he receives the angelic light as Tone from the higher worlds; he experiences a spiritual exaltation. The angels lift him beyond the portals of death, and the Love of God is open to him.

When there has been a close and tender relationship between the one dead and one who grieves for him in the physical world, the music of heaven is sometimes heard during the first three days after death by the one who grieves. This music, when it is heard by the living, removes the heavier pangs of sorrow, and permanently etches into the thoughts of the living the wisdom of death and the knowledge of eternal life.

THE SILVER CORD

There are three cords or threads of life: the umbilical cord, the silver cord, and the archetypal cord. The umbilical cord sustains

the life of the embryo during the period of
gestation and pre-birth. The silver cord or
soul's cord enables man to release his everlasting body from his physical body at night
during sleep, and it is also the means by which
he withdraws from the physical body at death.
The archetypal cord or spiritual cord determines one's response to Spirit, and works
with the soul to determine the length of life.

The silver cord, consisting of a veil-like
magnetic and etheric substance, has five antenna points. These points are correlated to
the spleen, the liver, the heart, the throat, and
the crown of the head. The mood for approaching death begins in man by the relax-
ing of the silver cord. During the first three
days after death, the silver cord is loosened
and withdrawn from its five antenna points.

*Or ever the silver cord be loosed . . . Then
shall the dust return to the earth as it was: and
the spirit shall return unto God who gave it.*

—Ecclesiastes 12:6,7

The archetypal cord or thread is the connecting link between Spirit and soul. This

cord has a heavenly consistency and vibrancy called a *hum*. The hum of the archetypal cord sustains the true identity of the spiritual self. When the hum of the archetypal cord decreases, the silver cord loosens its meshlike hold upon the spleen, and slackens its attachment to the liver; and the silver cord's tendrils, upholding the flame of life within the heart, are relaxed. With the decrease of the archetypal hum, the physical body begins to disintegrate, and the person, regardless of age, enters a dying state.

The soul's record of past lives and the record of deeds in the present life determine the length of life and the timing of death. The archetypal cord, working with the record of the soul, withdraws its hum when the purpose of one's life is completed. Whether one dies as an infant or in full maturity, he has fulfilled God's equation in some manner. Even though the promise of one's expression may appear to be incomplete, the person has answered and responded to the demands of the soul's record.

> *To every thing there is a season, and a time*
> *to every purpose under the heaven: A time to*
> *be born, and a time to die . . .*
> —Ecclesiastes 3:1,2

For three days after death, an activity still exists between the soul and the body. This activity is of uttermost importance to the Spirit of man. Even as the Lord Jesus required three days in the tomb to assemble His everlasting body, so does each person who has died require a three-day interim of repose and retrospection.

> *And He began to teach them, that the Son of*
> *man must suffer many things, and be rejected*
> *of the elders, and of the chief priests, and*
> *scribes, and be killed, and after three days arise*
> *again.*
> —St. Mark 8:31

The three-day interim after death is called interim-purgatory. These three days are a short interval in world time; yet, through the magnification power of his soul, one relives all of the events which occurred in the life just relinquished.

In the first 24 hours after death, the silver

cord or soul's cord is withdrawn from the spleen. With the help of the soul and the Recording Angel, the one who has died relives his ancestral memories. He re-enacts in his feelings and thoughts his attitudes toward his former kinship and ancestral ties. If one has had a stormy life of aggression and force, the sound he hears during the first 24 hours of interim-purgatory is discordant and oppressive. From this sound are reproduced pictures of his ancestral associations and relatives. The soul gives him a magnification of the senses through which he relives his procreative acts and sexual imaging; he discerns whether he has used his senses in a lustful or a reverent manner.

In the first 24 hours after death, Nature prepares the physical or earth body to be received back into the bosom of the earth. Those who die with restless wills, discontent, and with sensual desires unfulfilled, must contend with Nature; for they are unwilling to relinquish to Nature the physical body—the body they so loved while living in the world. Nature, which has fed, nourished, and given

physical sustenance to the physical body, turns
upon those who have led gluttonous and sensuous lives; and, in the first 24 hours after
death, sensual persons undergo the furies of
Nature. Their senses and their imaginations
experience the tumultuous and more violent
aspects of Nature. Nature creates a holocaust
of noise. The discordant and oppressive sounds
playing upon their senses give them the im-
pression that they are caught into storms,
cataclysms, hurricanes, and great winds.

Persons who have lived close to the heart
of Nature, and have loved her for her fruits,
her good, her warmth, and for her beauty,
willingly relinquish their physical bodies to
Nature with love. In the first day after death,
such persons make a covenant with Nature for
the next birth. In the coming life on earth,
they find themselves in beautiful environments
of Nature, where they are endowed with her
protection, blessings, and mercy.

In the second day, or second 24-hour period
after death, the silver cord withdraws from
the liver. The tone, music or sound playing

upon the one who has died is absorbed in a background theme, stirring the emotions and thoughts, and producing a mood of deep inner reflection. The soul enables the one who has died to magnify his former emotions and desires. His resentments, wishes, and hopes are enlarged and imprinted upon his thoughts. And he is given the opportunity to weigh and judge his motives. If one has loved himself rather than others, he suffers a form of self-pity. If he has used his will destructively in the life just lived, he suffers poignant regrets for waste of time and will. If one has lived an orderly and good life, his feelings and thoughts overflow with gratitude for the goodness and mercy in the world. If one has lived a pure, spiritual life, his expanding love penetrates the hearts and thoughts of the intimate ones he has left in the world. His love showers upon them as a tangible reassurance of his eternal being; for, in this second 24-hour interval, one who is spiritually evolved confirms all that he has believed and known of the immortal world.

In the third 24-hour interval after death,

the silver cord is withdrawn from its antenna
points within the heart, the throat, and the
crown of the head. In this period, the sacred
atom of the heart, which survives death,
unites with the pulsation of the soul; thus, the
everlasting or spiritual body is quickened and
prepared for its experience in the life after
death.

> *There is a natural body, and there is a spirit-*
> *ual body.*
>
> 1 Corinthians 15:44

During the last 24 hours of interim-purgatory, the loving works of one's life are weighed
upon the scales of the heart. If one has lived
vitally, hopefully, and lovingly, the love-
images and love-yearnings well upward when
the silver cord is withdrawn from the heart.
The one dead is enabled to see that love is
the greatest power in the world. In this interval, he is literally immersed in a sea of love.
His past anguish and pain are eased by the
balm of love which pours upon him. When
one does not have love within himself, he
cannot respond to the love of heaven; there-

fore, he fails to be elevated or lifted by the supporting and enveloping power of love.

In death, or life, men remember only what they experience consciously. The capacity to love determines one's degree of consciousness during the third day of interim-purgatory. If one has shut away his conscience during life, and has lived for self alone, he is unable to undergo the last 24 hours of interim-purgatory with awareness. It is God's merciful plan that persons with hardened hearts and atheistic minds sink into a frozen sleep and become immobilized during the third day of interim-purgatory; for the reviewal of their erroneous beliefs and misplaced actions is too painful for them to bear.

The sound sent forth from the soul is unheard by one who experiences the frozen sleep or mercy slumber. However, he is bathed in a mighty crescendo of sound. The sound renders him unconscious, and his last 24 hours in interim-purgatory are spent in a vacuum-like amnesia. Those who undergo the frozen sleep during the third day of interim-purgatory will fail, in coming lives, to recollect or to

intuit a life after death; and they will not have
a communion with the love-meaning of God.
Such persons are born to the world in the next
life with a belief solely in the reliability of
the senses and in what they can obtain in the
physical world. They believe that the physical
world is the only world, and they devote themselves solely to material things.

When one is unable to face his conscience
after death, and is atheistic or unbelieving,
the experience of the last 24 hours of interim-
purgatory is uncomprehended and sifts downward into the subconscious memory, which is
the lower pendulum of the soul. In lives yet
unlived, the reproaches of the conscience will
be re-awakened.

All who are unable to have total awareness
during the third day of interim-purgatory experience one of four different kinds of sleep:
(1) the frozen sleep or mercy slumber; (2)
the coma-like sleep; (3) the dreamlike sleep;
and (4) the bliss sleep. If one fails, in the last
24 hours of interim-purgatory, to record his
heart's actions and refuses to accept what his

conscience says, he sinks into a frozen sleep. One who believes not in an afterlife enters into a coma-like sleep. One who believes God to be but a Cause or a Law experiences the last day of interim-purgatory in a dreamlike sleep.

If one has believed that all men live repeated lives, but has failed to use the spiritual attribute of this belief while on earth, he is unable to rationalize heaven's impact upon him in the memory-retention period of the last 24 hours of interim-purgatory. He falls into the dreamlike sleep, and he undergoes the final day of interim-purgatory as a shadowlike inference upon the subconscious levels of the thought.

Persons who have obeyed the moral laws, but have not been initial doers of the good, experience the last day of interim-purgatory in the dreamlike sleep. During the last 24 hours of interim-purgatory, they are united with the grace earned through their obedience and through their recognition of protective laws of good. In the next life on earth, such persons will contribute to the good in the world.

The innately good person, who has inspired
others to do good, experiences the third day
of interim-purgatory in a bliss sleep. The bliss
sleep is an inducted rapture given of the soul.
In this sleep, he is united with the good works
of his just previous life. In his coming life on
earth, he will bring to the world a reverent
understanding, assuring men of the goodness
of God.

All who sleep during the third day of interim-purgatory will be unable to consciously
remember in the next life what occurred to
them in the after-death experience; thus, they
will be unable to recollect that men live after
death. This is the reason why so many people
in the world fail to have absolute knowledge
of a life after death, and of repeated lives.

In the next physical life, those who slept
during the third day of interim-purgatory will
have to rely upon the remembered emotional
and mental mechanics retained from their past
lives. Some will be uncertain as to eternal life
and God; others will intuit there is a life after

death, but they will be vague as to what one undergoes after death.

The last day of interim-purgatory is known in the higher worlds as the *day of retention*. Persons who are awake and aware of the third day of interim-purgatory have the power of retention, and return to the world with remembrance of heaven and of man's immortal destiny. While living on earth, they think through the poetic, the creative, and the spiritual aspects of the soul; and they live as beings rather than personalities.

Those who believe in God, in an afterlife, and in repeated earth lives, and who live godly and sacrificial lives while on earth, experience the three 24-hour intervals of interim-purgatory in full consciousness and awareness. After death, such persons are communicable to the powers of spiritual mediation working with them. In the last day of interim-purgatory, they align themselves with the pure works of the past life—works they have fulfilled without thought of reward. During these hours, they also are united with the pure, composite grace of former lives. This grace enables the Pure Dead to experience the next phase of purgatory—the 90-day contrition interval—in a different manner than those who slept through the third day of interim-purgatory.

The Pure Dead, the Saintly Dead, and the Elect Dead gain increased spiritual volume in their works after death; and, in the three days after death, they have a very special anointing power. A Saint, in his three days of introspection after death, conjoins himself with the grace of the world extracted from the pure and selfless works of humanity. The death of a Saint gives to the outer world a divine blessing, which is felt for thousands of years.

When the Elect, the Sacred Men, and the Saviours of the world die, in the three days after death they become catalysts of light to the earth. Having nothing to overcome after death, they are communicable to the faith of the masses, and they are in telepathic rapport with all spiritual persons—a rapport accentuated by their immortal victory over death.

Behold, I shew you a mystery; We shall not all sleep, but we shall all be changed. In a moment, in the twinkling of an eye, at the last trump: for the trumpet shall sound, and the dead shall be raised incorruptible, and we shall be changed. For this corruptible must put on incorruption, and this mortal must put on immortality. So when this corruptible shall have put on immortality, then shall be brought to pass the saying that is written, Death is swallowed up in victory.

—1 Corinthians 15:51-54

4.

TELEPATHY BETWEEN THE DEAD AND THE LIVING

When the piteous tears fall into the heart as pelting rain, and the clouds obscuring the light of the soul reveal the first hint of the rainbow of hope, one has entered the state of contrition and of a rebirth to the soul. The struggles of man are long, hard. He must learn to combine the dutiful with the joyful, the beautiful with the useful. He must shut not away his heart, nor blind himself to the truth concealed in each thing. He who is untrue to himself torments himself, but he who looks upon Light as the way will keep the upward look. He will give rhapsody to words yet inarticulate, and rapture to love yet unknown.

There are definite steps of progression and upliftment in the life after death. If one responds to the rhythmic progress offered in the afterlife, his soul enables him to experience a prolonged magnification of his conscience after the third day of interim-purgatory. In the higher worlds, this prolonged magnification of the conscience is called *the 90-day contrition interval*. For 90 days the one dead is given the opportunity to overcome self-justification, to seek forgiveness from the living for his impure, unthinking works, and to mend the scars of past associations through repentance and contrition.

When one is contrite in the 90-day contrition interval, the scales of the mortal vision are removed, and he stands in the incorruptible light of the after-death observation. He sees himself as one who has tried, but, in many ways has refused to live to the uttermost that which life has offered.

Contrition is not a state of torment. Contrition is a uniting of the conscience with the vision of the soul. Contrition is the desire to make right the wrong one has done; for no one can right the wrong he has done, save himself. Even as wrongdoing was done by self alone, so also must rightdoing be done by self alone.

One of the greatest fears a person has in the physical world is that his faults will be publicly exposed, and that he will be brought to account for his errors. If a person has had a conscience while living in the physical world, the secrets of his heart are laid open during the 90-day contrition interval after death. During this period, he feels and thinks through his conscience. All of the circumstances, the activities, and the intimate associations of the just past life are mirrored to him. His heart becomes filled with a burning desire to be contrite and to rectify his wrong works and acts. He yearns to be forgiven. He sees the waste of his former errors, and he holds himself accountable for his wrong works. The expansion of his conscience makes him feel that he must come close to those whom he has wronged in the physical world, and receive their forgiveness; he is possessed with the idea that only in this manner may he go on to the greater light awaiting him in the after-death state.

In this period of after-death sensitivity, the

soul gives the contrite person the power to make telepathic rapport with the minds of those he has known in his just previous life. His thoughts are telepathically inducted upon the thoughts of those whom he has loved or hated while living in the world. The 90-day contrition interval enables one who is contrite after death to rectify previous actions and to permanently detach himself from claim upon persons yet living in the world.

Those who grieve for the dead may notice, for approximately 90 days after the death of a loved one, that their thoughts are continually upon the one who has died. There are flashbacks of joyful memories and of seemingly inalterable regrets. The 90-day contrition interval is a blessing from God for both the dead and the living; for, in this exchange of thoughts between the dead and the living, past painful happenings are forgiven, much is understood—and more, something of grace is extracted between the dead and the living. A peaceful, comforting balm pours into the minds of those grieving, and the person dead is free to arise to the next sphere of action.

*I have seen his ways, and will heal him: I
will lead him also, and restore comforts unto
him and to his mourners.*

—Isaiah 57:18

The angels and the Men in White Apparel
work to educate those grieving in the world,
so that they may understand and take part in
the telepathic induction during the 90-day
contrition interval after death—the period in
which the thoughts of the dead and the
thoughts of the living must unite to accomplish
rectification as to that which exists in love or
hate.

If the one dead is completely contrite about
his wrongdoing, he does not repeat the same
mistakes in the coming life. Total contrition
enables a person to enter the next life free of
his former mistakes, and also enables him,
after death, to become one of the risen dead.

When a person is merely regretful or remorseful after death, and fails to be wholly
contrite, he becomes one of the unrisen dead;
in future lives, he must make retribution for
his wrong acts and errors of the previous life.
If he is unable, during the 90-day contrition

interval, to receive forgiveness from each person he has wronged in the physical world, he will meet them in some future life; and it will be necessary for him to rectify his mistakes under similar circumstances. In a coming life, he will attract to himself certain disciplines, whereby he may set aright that which he failed to acknowledge and accept in this 90-day contrition interval.

If the dead fail to be contrite, and still feel self-justified as to their wrong acts, they will reproduce their enmities and prejudices in the next life. If one is uncontrite during the 90-day contrition interval, and refuses to review the results of his former corrupt works and dissipation, he will enter the world in the next life sensuously inclined.

When the one dead acknowledges his errors, and is willing to receive instruction from the Men in White Apparel, he is enabled to build into his conscience and thoughts an accentuation of the inner soul-faculties, so that in the coming life on earth, he will have a closer relationship with his soul than he had in the just previous life.

If one believes in repeated lives, and has a contrite heart, the 90-day contrition interval is a rare experience of rationalization; for the soul opens to him the records of his former lives. He reviews his former lives and the motives of his former lives. His soul enables him to correlate the relevant past lives with the just past life. He comes to understand the former-life associations and placement. He can see why certain persons were in his life, and he can also see why certain obstacles were presented to him while he was living in the world.

If a person living in the world longs for death so that he may be reunited with someone whom he has possessively loved—and his thoughts are more upon the one dead than the living—the possessive person, during the 90-day contrition interval after his death, is unable to telepathically communicate with the living; for, in the after-death state, his thoughts are still upon the dead rather than the living.

A person who is contrite after death suffers intensely when his thoughts of contrition cannot penetrate the thoughts of those living in the world. During the 90-day contrition interval, he repeatedly implores the living to forgive him, so that his mind may be at peace, and that he may be free to respond to the instruction of the Men in White Apparel.

When an atheist loses some intimate person by death, and deliberately shuts his thoughts away from the thoughts of the one dead, the one who has died, being more sensitive than the atheist, suffers a terrible anguish; for his desire to rectify his past actions is frustrated and defeated.

Men unknowingly have the power to curse; that is, the power to *fix* an idea of hate. If one living in the world continues his hate for the one dead, this condemns the one living and the one who has died to a painful association with each other in a future life on earth.

When Jesus was in the throes of death and said, *"Father, forgive them; for they know not what they do"* (St. Luke 23:34), He gave to all men the example of blessing rather

than cursing. This exalted forgiveness freed
Jesus for the last step of overcoming or re-
leasing from the physical world. Thus, forgiveness must be between the dead and the
living.

The familiar saying, "Speak well of the
dead," is connected with the 90-day contrition
interval. Thoughts of condemnation by the
living intrude upon the after-death experience of the dead, and interfere with the work
and help of the Men in White Apparel. When
men classify the soul as being beyond redemp-
tion, this is a form of cursing.

The living, through their prayers and forgiveness, release themselves from the dead
and assist the dead to rise. Prayers for the
souls of those who die in mortal sin, without
repentance, are a prudent and wise necessity.
Pity for those who have erred, compassion
for those who have willfully wasted their
lives, and forgiveness for those who have
sinned help the erring dead to come closer
to the mercy of God. When men pray for

desolate souls, their prayers become a supplement to the works of heaven.

To hold bitter thoughts against the dead is to involve oneself in the telepathic concern of the dead. If the one living retains a resentment against the dead, he becomes receptive to a soiled magnetism exuding from the reproachful and regretful thoughts of the dead. Such persons often dream exhausting dreams of the dead, and awaken on the morning with something unfinished, painful, and unpleasant lingering in their emotions and thought.

A child or a young person, who dies before reaching the age of moral conscience, undergoes the 90-day contrition interval in a different manner. If the child has been of the risen dead previous to birth, he spends the 90-day contrition interval with the risen dead; and, with the help of his angels, he gives healing comfort to his parents.

A child, who has been of the earthbound dead previous to birth, enters the world with unruly and delinquent tendencies. If the child begins to repeat the same delinquency in adolescent years, and suffers death by accident, violence, or sickness, death does not expiate his errors. He experiences the 90-day contrition interval after death in a more sensitive manner than he did in the time previous to this life when, after death, he refused to be contrite for his delinquent acts.

When an adult does not offend outwardly the pattern of society, but lives with a rebellious spirit against life, he invariably attracts persons who are negative counterparts of himself. One who sorrows for an amoral, perverted, or criminal person who has died usually feels that death has solved the problem, and is the final and conclusive answer to a painful situation. Nothing could be further from the truth. While the person in the world is relieved by the absence of the physical presence of the one dead, and the unhealthy distractions caused by such association, the tie between the living and the dead is of even greater moral concern. The amoral dead, not having the conscience to benefit by the 90-day contrition interval, become even more burdensome upon the thoughts of the living.

A living person, who felt morally responsible for an amoral, perverted, or criminal person who has died, has the power to make the 90-day contrition interval easier for the one dead. If there be understanding, charity, and forgiveness in the heart of the living, the Guardian Angel of the erring or evil dead will surround and encase the one dead with bars of light, thus insulating the living from the telepathic thoughts of the evil dead.

During life, the neurotic, the psychotic, and the insane cannot control their emotions and thoughts due to a psychic injury to the silver cord. Having abused the mental will over a period of many lives, they have produced an imbalance between the will, the soul, and the thought. In the after-death experience, these confused persons are unable to coordinate their soul-faculties with their thoughts. During the 90-day contrition interval, they are prevented from communicating telepathically with the living.

The after-death progression for the mentally disturbed is a release from the nightmares of maladjustment. The neurotic, the psychotic, and the mentally deranged sink below the reach of the subconscious mind, so that the hallucinatory power of the subconscious mind is unable to reach them. The mercy aspect of God shields the mentally incompetent after death until the time when they can respond, consciously, to what their souls would say to them.

The mercy of God sends forth helps from the heavenly presences to heal the wounds of those who have harmed themselves through disobedience and unknowing. After death, the mentally disturbed are enveloped in cocoon-like encasements of light, and their personal angels watch over them and enfold them in mending love.

Some persons think a creative form of art belongs solely to themselves. No one creates singly in the world; men who create make up a composite whole. The creative dead and the creative living, when at one with the Will of God, are inseparable. Those who have cast aside the body to inhabit the immortal temples of heaven work continually to inspire the living to image, to mold, to form, and to give soul-life to that which shapes beneath the hand.

Persons who are part genius and heavily egotistical find themselves in the caverns of glamor during the 90-day contrition interval. Fragments of form and shape move against their thoughts and feelings in a kaleidoscopic manner. They behold patterns and designs of surrealistic nature. These surrealistic forms are projections from their own partly formed creations of the just relinquished life.

In the 90-day contrition interval, it is revealed to the egotist that what he had identified as being his own was, in reality, but a fragment of the whole; and that no one can claim his art or his genius to be wholly of himself. His 90-day contrition interval experience is one of purging, demoting, and deflating. His thoughts move downward to the earth in a form of shamefaced confession to those he has known. He feels a deep desire to return to the world, that he might express a true freedom in creation. He looks back upon his former egotistical claims as a form of insanity. His recognition of the ethic in creation will give him *carte blanche* in the next life; and he will achieve more resilience as to his purpose, and more humility as to his claim.

The soul's light of the pure poet enables him to enter the ecstatic and rapturous realm of the Cherubim Angels during the 90-day contrition interval. He learns of the origin of music. He learns the true purpose in the poetic phrase. He also observes the power of literature and of the written word. He is exalted in this experience because he sees the mighty working of the angelic host who assist the creative fiat within the soul of man.

If the poet is too ecstatic in the Cherubim Realm, his desire to remain in this blisslike state may detain him and upset the rhythm of the after-death progression. His personal angels watch over him and shepherd him upward toward the world of the risen dead, that he might begin his work in heaven, where as one of the risen dead he may work with the Illuminati. The Illuminati, right-hand companions of the Men in White Apparel, have achieved immortality on earth. Their work is to inspire the poets, the musicians, the writers, and the artists of the world.

The 90-day absorption of bliss by the poet is sent forth telepathically to the pure, poetic souls living in the earth. Often, works of art, new themes in music, and original ideas for sculpture are begun immediately after a pure poet leaves the earth; for the after-death bliss of the pure poet and his ecstatic experience in the Cherubim Realm accelerate the craving to create in the hearts of those living in the world. Thus, new forms are born when old forms die, proving that creation is deathless, and that life is immortal.

Pure persons who have been persecuted and victimized by prejudice, violence and hate are given, after death, a holy insulation against the evil thoughts of the living. These pure persons, having no errors to expiate, spend the 90 days of the contrition interval in a holy confirming of the mightiness of heaven, of the greater presences of heaven, and of the reality of the immortal purpose for all men.

The loving and pure dead leave their loved

ones with a *touch of grace*. In the 90-day contrition interval, the good dead pour their
thoughts as a golden rain upon those whom
they love. The pure dead shower blessings
upon those in the world who shared with them
the spiritual life. Their extended powers also
enable them to give forth a grace-blessing to
those they have known who are weighted down
with heavy burdens. A grace-blessing from the
pure dead has the power to transform the life
of the recipient, especially when there has
been love between the one living and the one
who has died.

A person close to sainthood experiences an
uninterrupted magnification of his spiritual
powers during the 90-day contrition interval
after death. He is able to give insight to the
minds of those who are blind to the eternal
laws and to the love of God. He also is able
to stir and to kindle the faith of those who
intuit the reality of heaven.

The Elect, the Saints, and the Saviours,
having no need to be contrite for their works
on earth, remain in proximity to the earth

during the 90-day contrition interval. They give their blessings to the world, reassuring men of immortality. A holy aroma, emanating from their ascension in death, enters into the naive, pure hearts of those bearing burdens in the world.

5.

THE UNRISEN DEAD

The atmosphere in the world of death has its latitude and longitude as related to the soul. The more man knows of his soul, the greater will be his experience after death. Death is a natural process, which neither stems from man's conclusions nor man's reasonings, but which stems from things as they are. When the soul's light functions as light, one is of the risen dead. When the soul's light functions as fire, one is of the unrisen dead in a state of purging or purgatory.

The purgatorial world is the world-subconscious. One experiences the heavier stages of purgatory with his subconscious mind. Hell in the after-death state is the subconscious mind unleashed.

Purgatory has a mathematical theme of discordance. This 'mathematical theme is to break down and destroy the old patterns in

which men have existed. Only the valiant and
pure may move over the panorama of purgatory.

When one lives in the physical world, he
depends upon his senses to observe and to experience. One undergoes the 90-day contrition
interval after death with his senses, his conscience, and his soul. How one responds to
the 90-day contrition interval determines
whether he becomes one of the unrisen dead
or the risen dead. When one fails to be contrite, and does not die to his lower emotions
during the 90-day contrition interval, he becomes one of the unrisen dead. He enters into
a lengthy purgatorial state, during which his
senses, his thoughts, and his emotions are experienced through the subconscious mind.

The earthbound dead are interested only in
the world of the living. Their senses, emotions,
and thoughts, still reaching toward the earth,
are unable to record the world of the dead, or
to understand its impact upon them. The unrisen dead, who are not earthbound, are aware
of the after-death caverns of purgatory. They
also are aware of others who are of the un-

risen dead. The purgatorial experience for the unrisen dead is divided into four activities: (1) periods of absorption wherein one responds to environment and instruction; (2) periods of hallucination during which his hidden, primitive aggressions are unleashed; (3) periods of anesthesia induced by music, causing a form of static rest; and (4) periods of deep sleep accompanied by dreams.

A gravity, called *the subtle-gravity,* exists in the subterranean caverns where dwell the unrisen dead. The subtle-gravity of the purgatorial caverns determines where the unrisen dead are placed in the after-death state. The subtle-gravity reaches forth and draws the unrisen dead to the purgatorial caverns or canyons where they will absorb, observe, and learn that which their souls would teach them.

Before the coming of Jesus, all men—with the exception of the Prophets, the Saints, and the Elect—slept through the various purgatorial stages. When Jesus was resurrected, He made it possible for men to ascend into higher degrees of light after death; He made it possible for men to imprint and record the memory of purgatory upon their subconscious minds and their consciences. He also enabled those who have pure hearts to become the risen dead.

Only since the coming of Jesus have men had the opportunity to undergo a "second death". The second death is the dying to the unruly, sullied and soiled emotions, and to the aggressive will. The majority of men in the world are unable to avoid the second death. All persons, with the exception of the pure, the Saints, the Elect, and the Saviours, undergo the second death after dying to the physical world.

> *Blessed and holy is he that hath part in the first resurrection: on such the second death hath no power . . .*
>
> —Revelation 20:6

The "first resurrection" is the first three days after death. When one is fully conscious during the three days of interim-purgatory after death, he "hath part in the first resurrection". The second death pertains to the 90-day contrition interval and to all purgatorial experiences thereafter. Some persons

overcome the second death in the 90-day contrition interval. If one has the grace to overcome the second death, he becomes one of the
risen dead. Others must remain in the purgatorial caverns of the unrisen dead until they
are ready to come back to the earth. Each
time a person dies, the lessons hc lcarns in
purgatory increase his capacity to overcome
the second death in forthcoming death experiences. In time, all men, with the exception
of the depraved, will have the power to overcome the second death.

Belief in God, in everlasting life, and response to the conscience, after death, enables
one to overcome the second death. When one
believes in God, His mercy and His justice,
he undergoes the 90-day contrition interval
as a quickening and rebirth to the soul. The
body of his lower emotions is sloughed off
and consumed by a fire proceeding out of the
lower octave of his soul's light.

If one is earthbound, his lower emotional
body becomes a vapor-like shell weighting
him to the earth. The unrisen dead, who are
not earthbound, are drawn downward by the

subtle-gravity pull into the purgatorial caverns which purge, cleanse, weigh, and adjust. The gravity-caverns of the subtle underworld magnify, reflect, and reproduce what one has felt and believed in the physical world.

Death is not a magic, making persons instantly good or pure. The emotions and the mentality are the same after death as they were in the physical world. If one has been atheistic in the emotions and thoughts, he is still atheistic after death; therefore, it is impossible for him to be contrite after death. His constant disbeliefs have immunized him to his conscience. After death, his conscience is paralyzed, and the 90-day contrition interval is blanked out from his consciousness.

Atheism is something which one has nurtured over a period of many lives. Atheism is the result of a gross and selfish heart. The atheist has been blind to his soul, and unaware of things spiritual in the world; after death, he also is blind to the accompanying presences in heaven. During the 90-day contrition interval, an atheist is unable to orient himself to the uplifting helps of heaven. Because of his hatred for things of the Spirit, on awakening after death he finds himself in the company of those who are also atheistic. The atheist and his companions are under the illusion that they still live in the physical world. They spend their time re-enacting with one another their sardonic and materialistic dramas.

The atheist spends the purgatorial experience in a desolate roaming; moving from cavern to cavern in the subtle underworld. This wandering may continue for an interminable time, until it gradually dawns on the atheist that he has died, and that death for him is but a magnification of his corrupt thoughts and feelings. On discovering that there is a life after death, the atheist remembers what had been said to him about eternal life when he was living on earth. Into his mind comes the horrifying thought that he must spend endless time in the shadowy caverns. He fears that he will remain in the darkened caverns forever.

The man that wandereth out of the way of

understanding shall remain in the congregation
of the dead.

—Proverbs 21:16

The length of time one stays in the subtle
underworld is determined by his belief, conception, and understanding of God. Because
the atheist has failed to believe in God, and
in a life after death, he is a laggard in the
afterlife. A laggard remains in the caverns
of the subtle underworld for lengthy periods
of time. To the minds of those who are confined in these caverns, time seems to be prolonged and endless. Thus, the atheist feels
himself to be a spectral automoton, caught
into the twilight caverns of the subtle underworld.

When the atheist realizes that he has been
his own enemy, and reaches a state of utter
despair, he begins his first response to his soul
and to the uplifting helps of the risen dead
and of the Men in White Apparel. He immediately receives the help of a Risen Dead
Preceptor, who has been atheistic himself in
some previous life. From this period on, the
atheist becomes an observer rather than a par-

ticipant in the caverns of the subtle underworld. The Risen Dead Preceptor, having
experienced former atheistic lives, is more
competent to give instruction and help to the
atheistic mind. This loving instruction relaxes
and changes the momentum of the purgatorial
experience of the atheist.

If an atheist's thoughts and feelings remain
infected with incredulity and doubt, and if
he fails to respond to the uplifting helps in
the afterlife, he is unable to reincarnate as
frequently as one who believes in God and in
a life after death. It is God's Plan that there
be neither repetition nor monotony in earth
or in heaven. In time, the atheist will be born
again, and he will be offered the opportunity
to find the meaning of life.

Those living in the world who grieve for an
atheistic person who has died suffer an anguish
without appeasement; for the atheist is unable
to penetrate their thoughts with love-assur-
ances of an afterlife. The living telepathically
absorb something of the desolate cavern experience. A desolation telepathy overflows into
the minds and thoughts of the ones who knew

and loved the atheistic person. For the living, this desolation telepathy continues for approximately 90 days after the death of the atheist. Thereafter, the telepathic bond between the living and the atheistic dead is sealed away— except for brief telepathic communications which occur in the minds and dreams of the living when the one who has died has some slight stirring upward towards the Light.

During the 90-day contrition interval, one who has lived a life of deliberate hypocrisy— giving an outer appearance of morality, but having a lustful and scheming heart—is drawn downward into the purgatorial cavern of mirrors. The heart and mind of a hypocrite are laid open in the purgatorial cavern of mirrors, where he sees reflected and mirrored back to him his scheming works and his cunning actions. If he is repelled by what he sees, he undergoes the remainder of the contrition interval in being regretful for his divided self; he makes a covenant with his soul to begin making retribution for his former hypocritical ways. In this period, through the help and instruction of the Men in White

Apparel, he is enabled to make some gesture of rectification for his past hypocrisies and deceptions.

If he becomes regretful, the hypocrite is able, telepathically, to reach those in the world he has schemed against and wronged. Persons living in the physical world who have been his dupes or victims often marvel to see some of the hopeless entanglements instigated by the hypocrite unravel as by an invisible hand. The lives of the victims, having been restrained and manipulated by the hypocrite, begin to express a pattern of order and justice. Thus, repentance and regret, if felt in the afterlife by the hypocrite, bring restitution to the living.

Even though the regretful hypocrite is possessed by an intense desire to be understood and forgiven, something within him tells him that time alone will make straight the crooked paths he has walked, and that rectification for his divided works will require many future lives of effort and ethic.

Paul the Apostle said, *"The love of money is the root of all evil"* (1 Timothy 6:10).

When one dies to the physical world, and dies not to miserliness, acrimony, avariciousness, and avidity, he finds himself in the purgatorial caverns of impoverishment. The Men in White Apparel work to teach the miserly heart the laws of universal equanimity and equation. In these caverns of impoverishment, the miser is taught that Nature hoards nothing, that her yield is lavish, abundant, and that he who hoards shuts himself away from the rhythmic timing or seasons within the law of supply.

A miser, after death, when faced with the coming life in which he must know lack and also must experience hard knocks, is reluctant to take up a coming birth. After death, much sleep or repose is undergone by a person with a miserly heart.

When one has been a confirmed miser, denying himself the first and decent necessities of life, such as clothing, food, and warmth, he has offended the law of receiving and giving. Having been obsessed with receiving rather than giving, he has shut himself away from his soul. In future lives, he will be the giver, and others shall take from him until he has set aright his offences against the law of justice and equation.

The miser, who refuses to give up his earthly possessions after death, becomes one of the earthbound dead. The earthbound miser, being unable to make rectification in purgatory, due to his love of earthly things, will haunt the environment of his possessions and hidden hoard. It is believed by some persons that when a ghost is seen, the one dead is protecting a secret treasure or hoard. This is no superstition; it is a reality—for the miser cannot detach himself from the only thing he loved and lived for in the just previous life.

All miserliness does not pertain to money. Those who hoard themselves, retreating from the demands of love, are also miserly. After death, they must review their miserliness in the caverns of impoverishment. To see themselves unloved, as they will be in some future life, produces a piteous anguish. Until such ungiving ones record in their souls the desire to give more, to love more, they will sleep; then, a tidal wave of reincarnation will pick

them up and draw them to the earth. Here
they will be provided with a loveless and
barren environment, offering to them in exact
justice what they have given in former lives
or times. All persons who have a desire to
retreat from the world should refrain from
hoarding themselves, so that they might avoid
coming lives of restraint and frustration.

There are some among the unrisen dead
who, while living, had mystical concepts of
heaven. After death, such persons find themselves in the glamor caverns of purgatory,
where they are able to literally reproduce their
ideas of heaven for a brief duration. Anything
one feels or thinks in the glamor caverns of
purgatory becomes pictorially real to him.
In the higher worlds, this is called *scene-shift-
ing*. Thus, such unrisen dead in the glamor
caverns are under the illusion that they have
reached the state of heaven.

Those who were thrill-seekers, or who
placed their trust in glamor while living in
the world, find themselves in the glamor caverns after death, wherein they experience a
buoyancy and prolonged giddiness, similar to

intoxication. For a brief period, one can will himself to rise, to fall, and to catapult. He becomes as a leaf blown by a knowing wind. If a person has loved sensation too much, he abandons himself to the buoyancy experience until he has exhausted this exuberant phase of *afterness.*

After one has undergone the glamor-cavern experience, and has saturated himself with the phantasy of his unrealistic beliefs, he enters into other caverns of instruction and envisioning. In the next phase of instruction, such persons find their emotions subdued, tempered, and cooled. The Men in White Apparel approach the unrealistic persons after death with the simplicity logic, teaching them the difference between wish and reality. When these persons are reborn to the world, they will be less subjected to phantasy, and their mental competence will be more astute.

If one has been unfaithful in the marriage relationship, his promiscuous sexual indulgence darkens his soul's record. In the after-death state, the adulterer must enter into the caverns of chastity, and learn of the sacredness of the procreative act. In the coming life, he will lack discrimination in the choice of a mate; for his soul's record will lead him to place his trust in some unchaste person, and to give his love to one who will be unfaithful to him.

When one has consented, through love, to the act of adultery, and becomes repentant and contrite while living in the world, he is able to unite with his soul during the 90-day contrition interval after death.

Jesus forgave the repentant harlot because, in looking into her heart, He saw that she had been a victim of the evils of society. Also, He erased the sins of the woman who "loved much".

> *Jesus saith unto them, Verily I say unto you, That the publicans and the harlots go into the kingdom of God before you.*
> —St. Matthew 21:31

Persons who were lecherous, lascivious, and lustful while living in the world are drawn downward after death by the subtle-gravity into the caverns of lust, where they observe the horrors of perversion and perversion's effect upon the soul of man. When such persons have concluded this painful experience, they are drawn by the subtle-gravity into the caverns of chastity, where they are shown the difference between passion and love. They are shown how, in many lives, they have deviated from pure love. They are taught that their underlying motive has been revenge against love. They also are shown that they have abused the greatest power given to man. The Men in White Apparel work with the lecher and the pervert to enable them to cleanse their defilement of love, and to accept their inevitable sexual impotence in coming lives.

The sensual, earthbound dead, who are blind and deaf to the higher helps after death, are attracted to lewd and corrupt physical environments. Sensual, earthbound entities have the power to insinuate their lewd and lustful desires upon the immoral living. They vicariously impose their sexual desires upon persons who are unclarified as to their own sexual desires. The sensual, earthbound dead siphon a sex magnetism from the lustful sexual acts of physical persons. This sex magnetism feeds and nourishes their lower emotional shells.

A depraved, earthbound entity has an octopus-like tentacle mechanism through which he may share and absorb the lust and sensual indulgences of men. The persistent intrusion from these earthbound entities degenerates the sexual vitality of their victims. They keep their victims from being reverent in their actions and influence them to be unfaithful in their love.

The earthbound dead, who have dulled their senses with alcohol or tobacco while living in the world, are attracted to familiar places, so that they may be warmed by human environments. Wherever there are darkened saloons, alcohol and tobacco, earthbound entities are near. Tobacco to the earthbound dead is similar to incense used in olden phallic temples. Such earthbound dead enjoy and saturate themselves in the aroma and fumes of alcohol and tobacco. Permanent alcoholics are often the victims of earthbound entity possession. Delirium tremens correlates to the hallucinatory caverns of purgatory.

Premature priests and precocious would-be celibates, who take celibate vows out of timing, offend the laws of propagation. The result is that the emotions and thoughts are colored by lechery and lust. Persons who force themselves to live celibate and austere lives must face their banked sexual desires in the after-death purgatorial experience in the caverns of lust. They remain in the caverns of lust for a brief time, after which they fall into a deep sleep within the caverns of chastity. In future lives, such persons have an aversion to marriage; and, if they enter the marriage state, they are unresponsive in their marital responsibilities. They make cold or lukewarm mates.

If one who lives a celibate life has yet to master his passional nature, he is not immune to the sexual temptations in the world. When he takes the vow of celibacy with a sensitive conscience, he undergoes something of the purgatorial fires while living in the world. He must continually die to his sexual desires while in the physical body. When such persons are free of the tensions produced by their sexual desires, they are exempt, after death, from the lust-cavern experience in purgatory.

The true celibate has concluded his procreative compulsions in former lives. When one makes the celibate's agreement with his soul in right timing, he has no difficulty in fulfilling celibacy.

> *But I speak this by permission, and not of commandment. For I would that all men were even as I myself. But every man hath his proper gift of God, one after this manner, and another after that. I say therefore to the unmarried and widows, It is good for them if they abide even as I. But if they cannot contain, let them marry: for it is better to marry than to burn.*
>
> —1 Corinthians 7:6-9

All persons who have offended the power of speech find themselves in the purgatorial cavern of silence. After the cavern-of-silence experience has concluded, the egotistical boaster, the smug and rabid conversationalist, the slanderer, the chatterer, and the liar are pulled downward by the subtle-gravity into the purgatorial canyon of echoes. In the canyon of echoes, one hears every word he has vainly or idly spoken. At first, he is fascinated and flattered by the words he has spoken throughout his life. Then he is appalled by the audacity of the thought in his words. Next he is aware that there was much he should not have said at all. He is aware that he has wielded the power of speech to wound and to harm. He is caught into rumblings and roarings of sound, which painfully reverberate upon him. Finally, he sees the futility and waste of his former words. He is astounded when he realizes how few of his words were kind, loving, or creative.

Following this experience in the canyon of echoes, all persons who have chattered without reason, or have slandered with vilification, or have spoken untruthful words are taken into the cavern of true words. They are taught that speech is a mighty power, and that there is a high destiny for a man with true words. They are taught that when speech is used destructively, it has the power to slay. When one responds to the purgatory instruction in the cavern of true words, he re-enters the world determined to speak true and to be true.

If one refuses to respond to the purgatorial instruction in the cavern of true words, in the next life he will be placed in environments with those who cannot and will not hear his words. If he has been a congenital liar, and is unremorseful in purgatory, in the coming life a restraint will be put upon his tongue; he will be unable to express himself through speech. If one has used words to slander others, he will be slandered and criticized in future lives.

The most intense anguish one may suffer after death is in the caverns of horizontal tumults within the lowest or sub-level depths of purgatory. The murderer must undergo these tumults. He who takes life through hate, deliberation, and an evil heart, must undergo the purgatorial tumults correlating to the bass tone of the earth. This purgatorial anguish is extended for lengthy intervals, until one drains off the violent aspect of the former murderous act. In the caverns of horizontal tumults, men say to themselves, "How long? How long?"

Those who die with blood on their hands

return to the world with a blood-guilt. Their souls determine how they must make retribution for the taking of life. Sometimes, a person with blood-guilt is caught into a web of circumstances in the next life, whereby he is convicted of—and executed for—a crime he has not committed.

Color, as well as music, plays a very important part in the afterlife. The Men in White Apparel and the angels who work with the dead use color therapy. The violent and unresponsive dead are immersed in colors ranging from the softest tints of the rainbow to the most somber shades.

The neurotic dead, the criminal dead, and the hardened dead are recipients of therapeutic music and color. Such persons, while undergoing the purgatorial anesthesia, receive color and music therapy. The color and music therapy is repeated over and over until the one dead is stirred by the desire to unite with the integral self, or the individuality residing within the soul. When the music and color therapy is concluded, he is given oral instruction by the Men in White Apparel.

Totally corrupt, evil persons who have lived for many lives as destroyers and persecutors of the innocent, and who have instigated slaughters and genocide, are withdrawn from the world of the living and from the world of the dead. They are withdrawn into a somber isolation, remaining in a submerged darkness, shut away from the light of their souls, and uncommunicable to the world. These evil persons are known as *the withdrawn dead*. When such persons die, they are beyond rectification, and do not return to the physical world. They remain in a frozen sleep, experiencing the death state in a chimeralike, twilight consciousness.

> *And cast ye the unprofitable servant into outer darkness: there shall be weeping and gnashing of teeth.*
>
> —St. Matthew 25:30

CAVERNS OF MERCY

Many persons commit wrongs due to ignorance, due to lack of discipline, and due to having been unloved. When death overtakes one who has been the victim of a sequence of neglects stemming from his environment, he experiences the 90-day contrition interval in the caverns of mercy, where he is given a tender, mending care; and the wounds of his uncertainties and insecurities are mended and healed. From time to time, the Men in White Apparel come to these hapless, wearied ones and instruct them as to their world within, and their place in God. Their lesson to learn, in the period between death and birth, is that the soul has the power to make man superior to his environment.

One of the greatest powers God has given to man is the power to rise above his environment—regardless of the environment. This is a power of the soul. When one denies this power, he denies his Creator. When the victory over environment is made through ruthlessness and selfishness, one becomes a doer of evil, rather than a doer of good; he frustrates himself and the plan of God.

In the mercy caverns of purgatory, the weary dead experience a cloudlike pictorial state of absorption. Their greatest sin on earth having been omission—that is, not doing—

they remain in the unrisen-dead state for a lengthy period of time after the 90-day contrition interval. The weary dead remain in the caverns of mercy until they are reborn to the earth in a civilization which holds the answer to their need. If they have responded to the Men in White Apparel in the mercy caverns, they will enter the world with triple responsibilities in the coming life, wherein they will exert their initiative, and experience the joy and gratification of works well done.

In the mercy caverns, the weary, inept dead are shown by example and observation the soul-records of great men who have mastered circumstances while living in the world. They are shown the miraculous power of overcoming, and its results in the world. Thus, the after-death experience for the weary dead is one of absorption, empathy, and emulation.

The weary dead cannot communicate with the living through telepathy during the 90-day contrition interval, for they are filled with a distaste for the life just relinquished. While living in the world, they did not have the capacity to understand the feelings and motives of others; therefore, after death, they are not interested in the world of the living.

Those living in the world who have neglected or abused the weary dead may receive regretful, recollective flashbacks in sleep or dreams during Christmas, Easter, the summer solstice, or the autumnal equinox.

One of the heaviest purgatorial experiences is that of dying to a creed or to certain fixed concepts as to the after-death reward or punishment. If a person is convinced that only a certain religious creed may place men in heaven, or if he believes that only through baptism can men be free from the purgatorial experience after death, he delays and hampers his progression in the after-death state. After death, such persons enter into the caverns of judgment, where they are shown the sacraments of the higher worlds overdirecting all religions. Here they learn that all religions are necessary in the world; they are taught that when a religion expresses the mercy aspect of God, a great good is rendered in the world. They also learn that religions which work not with the mercy of God, and which fail to interpret the laws of God with mercy and justice, are unaligned with the true ritual of heaven, whence stems all true worship. They are shown that such religions have power in worldly issues only, and have not the power to affect men after death.

When a person of devout religious beliefs receives a death sacrament in the last moments of life, there are certain tensions and fears removed from his mind. This is a blessing to many. If a person, who belongs to a religion requiring such observance, refuses the last sacrament, or by some circumstance finds it impossible to receive the sacrament, it is the destiny of this person to be free of that particular religion in the coming life on earth.

If one has united with his soul in the three days of interim-purgatory after death, earthly rituals have no power upon him; the heavenly rituals and the soul have supreme command. If a person be earthbound or in purgatory, pure prayers and rituals of a religious nature affect and help him.

The belief that children must be baptized to avoid purgatory after death is needlessly painful to parents who lose a child who was unbaptized before death. The belief that a child is bound for all eternity to the purgatorial worlds after death, if the child was not baptized in some special religion or creed, has no effect upon the dead, but has a painful effect upon the minds of the living.

Prisons and penal institutions in the world reflect certain purgatorial caverns. Jesus, after death, descended into purgatory and preached "unto the spirits in prison".

For Christ also hath once suffered for sins, the just for the unjust, that he might bring us to God, being put to death in the flesh, but quickened by the Spirit:

By which also he went and preached unto the spirits in prison.

—1 Peter 3:18,19

Men caught in their criminal acts in the physical world are fortunate, for they have the opportunity to purge away their crimes while imprisoned in the physical world. If they will repent, and be remorseful for their hates, lusts, and greed, which instigated their crimes, they will have a greater freedom after death. However, not all men who commit crimes are in penal institutions. Those who take from the weak, or deprive them of their monies and possessions—or who, through physical world authorities, prey upon and exploit their fellow men—find themselves after death in the criminal, isolation purgatory caverns. In these areas of purgatorial isolation and confinement, they have the opportunity to see that they are the victims of their own criminal acts.

> . . . *we are in desolate places as dead men.*
> —Isaiah 59:10

After death, those who have unrepentant, criminal hearts are taken into restraining areas in the purgatorial caverns; unless they have acquired occult powers in previous lives, they cannot escape the purgatorial isolation impressed upon them. Criminals who have had occult knowledge in former lives understand the working of the subterranean caverns of the dead. Thus, they have the power to refuse to accept isolation. Being remorseless, they take delight in preying upon the thoughts of criminally inclined persons on earth. Many crimes committed in the physical world are due to the suggestions and thoughts sent by the criminal, earthbound dead. The thoughts of an earthbound, evil person make an unholy impact upon the criminally inclined mind in the world.

When a hardened criminal is killed by the state, and he is unrepentant for his crimes, he becomes a menace to the living and to the dead. In time, the mercy of God will annul capital punishment. As men come closer and closer to the ethic of Jesus, they will understand that a state as well as a man should observe the Commandment, "Thou shalt not kill."

In the criminal, isolation caverns of purgatory, the Men in White Apparel are assisted by the Order of Jude. The Order of Jude consists of men who have lived in the physical world and who have in some manner lived close to crime; they have a unique understanding of the criminal heart and mind. The Order of Jude, wearing blue garments, works as an arm of the Men in White Apparel. The men in the Order of Jude work to keep before the criminal mind the mercy of God. They instruct, teach, and assist the criminal minds to accept the retributive disciplines which they are to assume in coming lives. The criminal dead who accept the instruction of the Order of Jude return to the world determined to rectify immoral intent. Such persons sometimes find themselves in positions of policemen, soldiers, judges, lawyers, and magistrates, or wherever there are penal institutions. They work sympathetically to reshape and to give hope to the criminally inclined; they seek to prevent crime through merciful and constructive methods.

People living in the world, who have been associated with the criminal dead, may aid and give spiritual help to those who are isolated in the purgatorial caverns due to earth crimes. Their prayers aid the Order of Jude to help the erring ones.

Forgiveness is greater than judgment. If one has a contrite heart, he receives the benefic blessing of forgiveness after death, as in the case of the contrite thief who was crucified alongside of the Lord Jesus. His acceptance of the justice meted out to him for his evil deeds, and his recognition of Jesus as the Saviour, enabled him to be with the Lord Jesus in paradise.

And Jesus said unto him, Verily I say unto thee, To day shalt thou be with me in paradise.
—St. Luke 23:43

Paradise is a peninsula or bar of heavenly light located between the purgatorial caverns and the First Heaven. All persons touch paradise after death. The wicked, being asleep, are unaware of paradise; the good are awake. Paradise is given of God, that all who die might experience for a brief time a preview of heaven. In paradise, there is beauty such as men have never seen on earth. There is incessant action, order, rightness, and no resistance. Paradise is every man's plateau—a pause after death to give one stamina for the next phase of progression following death.

Paradise is similar to a sandbar at sea. It is a springboard to either the darkened caverns of purgatory, or to the lighted corridors of heaven. On each side of paradise are whirling, intelligible currents which draw one to his rightful place. The Guardian Angel, working with the record of the soul, determines whether one crosses over the bar of paradise into purgatory, or into the First Heaven where dwell the risen dead.

6.

THE EARTHBOUND DEAD

Why do men dread death? Men dread not the dying; they dread the facing of the conscience, exposing their secret sins. The soul says to him who dies: "Come, look into the mirror of thyself. Scrutinize thy vanities, thy conceits, thy justifications, and thy logics. Put upon thyself the cloak of truth. Deny not what thou hast done; for, if thou didst bargain to err to learn, thy conscience shall not turn upon thee. If thou seest a good account of thy gifts, thou shalt rejoice; but if thou hast been a neglectful steward of thy gifts, thy better self will tell thee that thou must try and try again."

God is a God of love. God does not punish His children. The laws of God are etched into the soul of man. The conscience is the reflector of the laws of God. When a man errs in the physical world, the laws of God become a checkrein upon his actions. When he

97

deliberately refuses to listen to his conscience, he delays the consequential reaction resulting from his wrong actions—and his deviations are imprinted by his conscience upon the record of his soul. If the soul's record is heavily burdened with that of evil and wrongdoing, the one who dies is weighted downward toward the earth; thus, after death he is earthbound, and he is slow to respond to the uplifting helps of heaven. Ages may be consumed before an earthbound person is released from the earthbound state to finally complete the purgatorial experience. In some instances, the earthbound dead remain close to the earth for an interminable time.

The earthbound dead are of the lowest octave in the unrisen dead. However, not all earthbound persons are evil. Nonacceptance of the reality of death also may earthbind a person after death. Some earthbound persons were well-meaning previous to death; but, because of their unknowing of the afterlife and its progressions, they still linger close to the earth, refusing to accept the death state and a life after death.

The well-meaning and unknowing dead may be temporarily earthbound to earth memories, places, and associations. After their earthbound state is concluded, the well-meaning dead move into the caverns of the purgatorial world, where the Men in White Apparel teach them the difference between good and evil. After the well-meaning dead have completed their purgatorial experience, they become, by slow degrees, the *quickened dead*. This usually occurs just before their birth to the next life.

Before death, evil, earthbound persons expressed violent emotional compulsions. After death, their emotions become a raging torment to them. Being uncontrite, the evil, earthbound dead are unable to die to their lower emotions. Their unruly emotions compel them to seek out former environments and persons whom they either hated or dominated.

Earthbound persons have the power to appear to the living. Those who are unaware of the proximity of the earthbound dead are blessed by the mercy of God. If one living in the world has benefited materially by the physical-life evil conquests of the earthbound dead, or if he was a willing accessory to the evil earth works of the earthbound dead, he will be vulnerable to the will of the earthbound dead. The force of the harsh will of an evil, earthbound person, when felt by the living, produces an anomaly—and a fearful thing.

All earthbound persons undergo tides of anesthesia, which move over them in cycles or periods. These tides of anesthesia slacken their grip upon the world. When the violence in the will of an evil, earthbound person has abated, he undergoes a pre-birth anesthesia, and prepares to reincarnate or return to the earth.

The earthbound dead may commune with the living either through subversive telepathy or reproachful thoughts to the living—or through apparition or appearing to the living. An earthbound person can make himself known and seen by the living if he has a strong, unhealthy attachment to some unfinished incident, such as having been murdered or violently killed; or if he has an outraged sense of betrayal as to the use of his properties or possessions.

The body of the lower emotions, which the earthbound dead failed to consume in the fires of contrition, becomes an apparitional body, which can be seen by some persons living in the world. The apparitional, earthbound dead are often called "ghosts" by people living in the world. The spectral or apparitional, earthbound dead are confined to the cross currents between purgatory and earth. The earthbound dead, refusing to believe they have died, are blind and deaf to the helps of their angels; they can be reached only by the living. Prayer, accompanied by the knowledge of the true ritual for the dead, can exorcise and release the earthbound dead.

The apparitional dead can devitalize and harm the living. They also can use audible sound and the destructive after-death energies to produce frightening phenomena; for they have the power to quicken and to use the latent psychic, kinetic force in objects. Earthbound persons often take a cunning delight in disturbing a household or an environment. Their subverted emotions feed upon the fears of their victims.

The earthbound entity, having been conscienceless and parasitical while living in the earth, is parasitical after death, and preys upon the living. The satanic forces and principalities and powers of darkness work through the evil, earthbound dead. The powers of darkness utilize and exploit the dead who had corrupt hearts while living in the world. In the darkened caverns of the subtle underworld, subtle and wicked authorities prey upon the living who have any portion of malice, covetousness, greed, or lust.

Wickedness in high places, or in religious atmospheres, is inspired by earthbound, long-dead bigots. This wickedness is a projection of the Antichrist challenging the right of every man to worship his God.

> *For we wrestle not against flesh and blood, but against principalities, against powers, against the rulers of the darkness of this world, against spiritual wickedness in high places.*
>
> —Ephesians 6:12

The apparitional, earthbound dead, in their

vapor-like, wraith-shells, are attracted to old decaying buildings, swamps, or wherever there is a state of degenerate action. The earthbound dead also inhabit the darkened cabinets and seance rooms of mediums. The earthbound dead extract living, earth magnetisms from the physical bodies of those who seat themselves in raptured expectation of psychic phenomena. Such persons, who seek proof of a life after death, know not the dangers to which they expose themselves in such discarnate association.

Communion with the dead is inevitable, but wrong communion with the dead is a macabre practice, unhealthy for the living and inconvenient for the dead. Those who call up the dead, or engage in psychical inquiry into the realm of the dead, endanger themselves; for their ignorance of the spectral and apparitional phenomena brings upon them disaster and tragedy, affecting their mental, moral, and emotional equilibrium. The Biblical story of Saul, the witch of En-dor, and Samuel is one to be remembered by all who would call up the dead.

And Samuel said to Saul, Why hast thou dis-
quieted me, to bring me up?

—1 Samuel 28:15

To call up the dead produces an abnormal
thing in the world. To disturb the dead is an
act of intrusion upon the one who has died.
When one seeks to resolve some material problem in the earth by calling upon the dead, he
offends the ethic of prayer. All petitions for
help should be made to "Our Father which
art in heaven."

When Samuel rebelled against Saul's having the witch of En-dor "bring" him up, he
was in what is known as the Prophet's Sleep.
The Prophet's Sleep is a state of heavenly
absorption through which the prophet sees
things which have been and things which are
to be.

Any person who has an interest in psychic
phenomena, and indicates some tendency toward psychical powers, should follow to the
letter these two admonitions:

Beloved, believe not every spirit, but try the
spirits whether they are of God . . .

—1 John 4:1

Prove all things; hold fast that which is good.
                              —1 Thessalonians 5:21

Unless a person has an abnormal and insatiable curiosity, he will not remain allied with the psychical arts for any lengthy period; for his soul will develop in him a distaste and repugnance for that which continues to lead him into blind alleys. In placing his trust in the sullied denizens of the subtle underworld, he will receive grievous lessons, scars, and scorchings.

The earthbound entity is a menace to the life of the spiritual person. If one who seeks to live a spiritual life retains the slightest desire to obtain spiritual powers without effort and willing sacrifice, he falls victim to the earthbound entities of the subtle underworld.

After one has been earthbound for a long period, he develops certain antenna-like projections or tentacles of subtle ether by which he attaches himself to some unwitting and unknowing victim.

A person cannot be possessed by an earthbound entity unless he has, in some degree, a subjective nature. When one uses his will in right balance, he cannot be possessed by an earthbound entity. One who relinquishes his will to the dominant will of another, or has been subjected to the will of another through hypnosis, can become an *invitational field* for an earthbound entity. When one is consistently indecisive, he becomes a *neutral field* for the earthbound dead; he may be subjected to an earthbound entity of low caliber, or he may be subjected to an earthbound entity who possesses a higher form of intellect.

When one possesses psychical powers, and yields himself to persistent intrusion from earthbound entities—or, when one by wrong sentiment as to thoughts of the dead inadvertently opens the door to the earthbound dead—he makes of himself a household in which an earthbound entity may dwell. The earthbound entity sets up a series of barrages against the left side of the body of the one living; and, if the person has no means of protection, the entity eventually gains an entry. The earthbound entity literally crawls into the body of the person, and sets aside the vital thread connecting the ego and the soul of the one living.

The entity then takes possession of the brain of the person, and begins to think and act through his nervous system. From that time forward, the person living in the world is possessed. This is what the Scriptures mean by a person being "beside himself" (St. Mark 3:21).

When an entity-possessed person dies, the earthbound entity withdraws himself and seeks another victim through which he may function.

One living, who invites an entity to come into him, or consents to entity possession, becomes wholly devitalized as to his will and incapacitated as to his action. Such a person undergoes a death similar to a suicidal death. Having failed to express himself personally from the time the entity possessed him, he will find himself after death in a state of great confusion. It will require many lives of readjustment for him to return to an equilibrium or possession of his own will, and to the direction of his own acts.

The advanced psychiatrist of the future will understand man by placing an emphasis upon the soul, rather than upon the mind and the subconscious mind. He will come to see the difference between the obsessed person and the possessed person. Obsession is caused by the overshadowing of a former life. Possession is due to one's being possessed by an earthbound entity.

Obsession may occur during weakened or depressed periods in one's life. In obsession, one takes upon himself certain former-life characteristics, and there is a decided personality change.

When one has consistently used psychical power rather than spiritual power in the present life or in former lives, he becomes a vehicle for earthbound entity possession. This subjective entity state creates an obnoxious and ungodly thing in the world. It is a demoniac force driving a person to destroy and to harm. Only those having knowledge of the powers of the soul can exorcise such entities from the hapless victims who succumb to their evil possession.

And when he was come to the other side into
the country of the Gergesenes, there met him

*two possessed with devils, coming out of the
tombs, exceeding fierce, so that no man might
pass by that way.*

—St. Matthew 8:28

One of the ways a person may recognize
earthbound entity possession is by a condition
called *astral jaundice*. The skin of the subjective person develops a waxy, yellow pallor,
and the flesh beneath his eyes appears bruised,
having flecks of purple and brown. His feelings are listless, and his thoughts are depress-
ive, defeatist, and suicidal. He also experiences alternate states of delusions of grandeur,
egotism, and vanity. When an entity has taken
full possession, the subjective person will not
look anyone in the eyes. An unaccountable,
spasmodic jerking of the body is also indica-
tive of entity possession.

Earthbound entities cannot stand pure
water and cleanliness. They love disorder and
untidiness. Many crimes are instigated by
earthbound entity hypnosis. Crimes committed
without premeditation by immorally inclined
persons are often due to earthbound entity
possession. The earthbound dead are spoken

of in the Bible as the "unclean spirits". Jesus gave His disciples the power to cast out unclean spirits.

> *And when he had called unto him his twelve disciples, he gave them power against unclean spirits, to cast them out, and to heal all manner of sickness and all manner of disease.*
> —St. Matthew 10:1

The earthbound dead can linger near an animal and cause the animal to behave in a very peculiar manner. It is possible for an animal to see the dead before one is aware of the visitation of the dead.

Man is a speaking and thinking being; he has a reasoning intellect. Man has never lived in the form of an animal, and will never be an animal. When the earthbound dead fail to find a magnetic subjectivity to feed upon in an environment, they sometimes seek to attach themselves to the fluid in the spine or abdomen of an animal. From this stems the false belief in transmigration, that is, the belief that man may reincarnate as an animal.

The earthbound dead who refuse to respond to the purgatorial state, and who still cling to earth affections and interests, are often intruders against their former mates. In event of remarriage by the widowed person, this imposes a tremendous trial upon those newly married. If the one who is earthbound refuses to relinquish his or her claim to the physical possessions within the home and to the emotional ties sealed in from long years of association, the earthbound person may cause an abnormal triangle action, producing great unhappiness to the former mate. To those married and seeking a new beginning and happiness in life, the subtle jealousies of the earthbound dead endanger the marriage, causing conflict, confusion and, sometimes, separation. This unhealthy triangle is made possible because the one living is uncertain of his or her love for the second mate; or it may be caused by some unresolved debt incurred in the marriage state in a former life. True love between those newly married has the power to seal away the earthbound dead.

The earthbound dead do not see the physical actions or movements of the living. However, they sentiently penetrate the feelings, the motives, and the thoughts of persons who are sympathetic to them, or who have equal degrees of thought. An earthbound person can only penetrate a mind and thought similar or equal to his own. Thus, the sentient earthbound dead are drawn to the sentient motives and feelings of the living. The revengeful earthbound dead are attracted to persons of revengeful temperaments. The earthbound dead can also influence those who had been unnaturally dependent upon them while they (the earthbound dead) were living in the world.

The earthbound dead are repelled by pure love, by prayers, by clean and orderly atmospheres. It is impossible for the earthbound dead to interfere with the ethical industry of the living. It is impossible for the earthbound dead to penetrate persons with unfamiliar routines and habits. They are attracted only to familiar patterns, affinities, and associations previously experienced by them while living in the physical world.

There are some among the earthbound dead who do not intrude upon the living. These are known as the *observing entities*. The observing entities have an after-death wanderlust; they move from place to place unaware that they may rise. Having a restless inquisitiveness, they linger near earth environments. The wanderlust dead were materialistic persons who had neither emotional, mental, nor spiritual roots while living in the world.

Many of the priests of magic who lived in Persia, China, Chaldea, and Babylonia are still in the earthbound state. Any one with psychical powers may come under their domination. The earthbound dead, who have used perverted occult powers in previous lives, affect the living in an unholy manner. When one seeks to link himself with magical instruction from the dead, the result for the living is unwholesome, and produces amorality; for the magical powers of former ages are abnormal when one seeks to apply them in the present scientific age. The subtle directives from the earthbound, occult dead sap the judgment, dissipate the incentive, devitalize the physical energy, and shut away the ingenious inspiration of the soul.

Many East Indians, who practiced the lower phases of yoga during life, are earthbound (1) because they believed that their yoga and ascetic practices would enable them to be free from the wheel of rebirth, and (2) because they believed in a static state of life after death. The yogi, earthbound entities have strong and penetrable telepathic powers. As *astral gurus* they seek to impose their wills upon the unknowing in the physical world. Often, students who have reached a ripeness in metaphysics, and who are ready for the next step of initiation, undergo an initiatory challenge, in which they are exposed to the earthbound, astral gurus who pose as "Masters". If the students are mystically inclined, they think the psychical experience is a spiritual experience. If one consents to the instruction of the astral guru, his life begins to be supervised, psychically, by the earthbound yogi. The one living becomes fanatical as to his food and body habits. His practical life falls apart. Being possessed by the Eastern earthbound tutor, he seeks to live an Eastern life while living in the Western world.

There is a sardonic humor, mockery, and malice engendered from the astral guru labyrinths, for the satanic principalities work directly with the astral gurus. Thus, when a person becomes the dupe of an astral guru, there is glee of a satanic kind set up in the labyrinths where dwell these corrupt entities. Such entities sustain their life by living upon the magnetism and vitality of mediumistic and psychical persons in the physical world. The person who would live the spiritual life should seek to make himself pure in heart, so that he may rise above these subterranean forces.

The communication from the astral guru labyrinths may be likened to a contraclockwise dot-and-dash code which is sent in a continuous, insistent voice to those who are yet egotistical, acquisitive, careless, mystical. One may recognize the contraclockwise dot-and-dash system by (1) continued moods of depression, (2) a persistent, critical attitude toward other persons, (3) a desire for self-enlargement and grandeur, and (4) certain dreams which appeal to personal exaltation

and authority. Therefore, it may be seen by
the spiritual person how very necessary it is
to give of oneself without thought of gain,
claim, or recognition. At all times, one should
armor himself with Light and the works of
Light in the name of the Christ, seeking to do
the Will of the Father sincerely and conscien-
tiously. Only in this way will he be insulated
and protected from the subterranean, astral
dot-and-dash, psychical and inverted communication.

Investigators of the psychical regions, and
self-appointed metaphysical teachers, work
unknowingly with these psychical cohorts,
and draw their grandeur ideas from the subterranean corridors of the lower astral labyrinths. All persons who come under the tute-
lage of these subverted powers walk a dead-
end way, and must eventually retrace their
steps. Some persons waste many lives upon
the psychical treadmill.

The psychical powers exist. They may be
likened to raw electricity. When used harm-
fully, they will, in time, turn upon the person
and harm him. When one begins to insulate

himself spiritually, he will be protected from the crude depletions of a psychical atmosphere. Thus, the waste of time and thought, and blind obedience to the psychical planes will eventually be overcome when one truly dedicates himself to the pure, to the good.

Ouija boards, tarot cards, crystal balls, or any mechanical objects connected with the psychical arts are astral toys and trinkets. These may be used by an astral guru or another earthbound entity to penetrate the subjective mind, thereby taking possession of a person's will and manipulating him in a puppet-like fashion. If one has used occult powers in a negative manner in previous lives, he will be interested in occult powers to be gained through the use of astral toys.

Automatic writing, one of the psychical arts, invites an astral guru or an earthbound entity to take possession. Automatic writing separates and short-circuits the voluntary and involuntary nervous and muscular systems. When one becomes ' dependent upon automatic writing, and practices it over a long period, he opens the psychic portals to the subconscious mind, and endangers the mentality. His thought process becomes imbalanced, for he distorts the coherent alignment between the will, the memory, and the imagination.

When an astral guru or a spectral entity takes possession of a person living in the world, it may be truly said that the person can no longer call his soul his own.

A man's sexual frustrations and bitterness will open the door to entity possession. A woman's jealousy and impurity as to sexual outlook will open the door to entity possession.

Among the earthbound entities still lingering close to the earth are the degenerate egos who inhabited the Western Indian tribes during the latter Atlantean times. There are thousands of such earthbound Indians who refuse to reincarnate; due to their knowledge of former occult Atlantean laws, they are able to resist the tidal waves of reincarnation. Some persons in the physical world having mediumship powers fall victim to these discarnate, depraved Atlanteans, and become their sepulcher homes. The discarnate entity, over the years, gradually takes possession of the body and the nervous system of the medium; henceforth, the entity controls the senses, the wishes, and the desires of the medium.

When persons inclined toward the occult—who have delved into supersensory powers—travel to Egypt, they invite the interest of the earthbound priests of Egypt, particularly of the mortician-priests of the dead. The most prevalent earthbound state existing in the world today is in the Valley of the Kings in Egypt. Many of the old mortician-priests of the Egyptian dead, understanding the sub-etheric, occult laws, and also the laws of re-incarnation and re-embodiment, still linger in the environment of the Valley of the Kings in Egypt. Through their use of invocation, and their control of the etheric elemental creatures, the mortician-priests of ancient Egypt confined thousands of persons to an earthbound state—keeping them in a twilight sleep for ages, and preventing their rebirth to the world. When men began to desecrate the tombs of the dead in Egypt, they violated the protective precinct of the dead and offended the etheric elemental creatures; the earthbound mortician-priests and the elementals turned upon the intruders, often causing death or some terrifying, psychical experience.

Some of the mortician-priests of Egypt have reincarnated, and are living in the world today. They may be found in various parts of the earth, especially among those who are extremely interested in psychical phenomena. Such persons may be recognized by their knowledge of the anatomy of the body and by their occult interpretation and diagnosis of sickness and disease. These former mortician-priests, having been of the profane priesthood while living in Egypt, were sealed away from the knowledge to be gained from the higher Atlantean mysteries. In the present life, they are solely interested in occult powers and in the practice of phenomena. They are unable to understand the spiritual ethic accompanying the use of such powers; therefore, they are unable to assimilate the teachings of the Christ.

In ancient Egypt, those who were initiated into the higher Atlantean mysteries were enabled to break through the earthbound confinement of their tombs, and to reincarnate in the rhythmic timing needed by their souls. In the present age, the initiates who mastered the higher Atlantean mysteries carry the light for men in the world. They may be found wherever there is pure, spiritual leadership.

THE GRAVITY-BOUND DEAD

There are the extrovert dead and the introvert dead. The extrovert dead are the earthbound; the introvert dead are the gravitybound. Next to the suicide, the gravity-bound dead are the most pathetic of the dead.

Each life is timed to the need of earning and learning. One who wastes his time, his energy, and his wits in the physical world is a wastrel, and harms but himself. An apathetic physical life creates a vacuum in heaven. When such a person turns his face to heaven after death, he must face this vacuum.

The gravity-bound dead are the victims of their own inertia and of their own pallid feelings. Because their emotions are sterile, empty, or unfeeling, they are unable to respond to the prayers of the living and to the helps given in the world of the dead. The gravity-bound dead, having neither the feelings nor the conscience to be contrite for their former-life acts and works, are the immobile dead.

The inertia of the just previous physical life, exposed to the velocities of the purgatorial caverns, produces the tone of pain upon the antennas of consciousness. He who refuses to respond to life while in the physical body is a greater sinner and errs more than he who provokes the law through zeal and blind egotism; for when one is active in the physical world he has the opportunity to learn from errors. But when one refuses to be taught or to coordinate with the world in which he finds himself, he offends the Life Principle and the Law of God.

Each person is born in a certain era of time, a certain place, exposed to the laws of Nature, to personal environments, to society. If he fails to move with the tide of that offered to him, the result is remorse in heaven, and a lengthened or delayed period between births until he may return to earth again with vigor, expectation, and hope.

The after-death experience for a parasitical or apathetic person is supervised and directed by the Men in White Apparel for extended periods. Persons who enter the world of death devoid of spiritual treasures from the just past life fall into self-accusing contemplations for lengthy periods.

The gravity-bound person cannot communicate with the living; he is concerned solely with himself in the after-death experience. The subtle gravity of the purgatorial world sweeps him into the purgatorial caverns, where he undergoes a subtle induction to produce some animation in his feelings and conscience. What he has neglected in his emotions is accentuated and exaggerated in these caverns, so that eventually he may be quickened and, thereby, respond to the higher instruction awaiting him.

ANIMALS AFTER DEATH

Animals live after death. Animals also reincarnate. If a domestic animal is fond of a former master, its devotion to its master and love of its environment will earthbind the animal. However, this earthbound condition will prove helpful to its master, for the animal, after death, has a certain protective power. An animal after death, when protecting a former environment, can send a warning and an electrical charge against an intruder. However, in time, the Species Angels direct the animal which has died into another birth impulse, and the animal returns to the earth.

When animals reincarnate, they do not change their species. From life to life, they remain domestic or wild; a dog continues to be reborn in the canine species, and a cat in the feline species.

Until man domesticated certain animals, the Species Angels prevented the cross-breeding of species, keeping pure the breed. Since man took upon himself the responsibility of cross-breeding animals, domestic animals can be born in another breed, but the species of the animal remains the same. Thus, a fox terrier of the canine species may become in the next life another breed of canine, such as a bulldog.

Animals, being devoid of conscience, are free of after-death purgatorial experience.

When animals die, they are drawn into the animal-species matrix, which is overdwelt by the Species Angels and Fauna Angels. In this species matrix, animals absorb into themselves the meaning of the animal kingdom and its purpose in the world. They are shown by the Species Angels that their role in the physical world is a role of sacrifice. As men become more highly evolved, the wild species of the animal kingdom will disappear from the earth, and the domestic animals will become a greater rarity. Eventually, the Species Angels will withdraw all animals from the earth.

After death, wild animals absorb a revitalizing survival impulse to be used in the next life. Domestic animals, being familiar with the life-mechanics of men, sometimes linger with men in the caverns of the unrisen dead, and seek to make these places their home.

When an animal's master dies before the animal, a devoted animal's love for its master will enable it to join its master wherever he is in the life after death.

7.

THE QUICKENED DEAD

The records of the scrolls of death are read in deep blue light by him who prepares to become one of the quickened dead. In the Pavilions of Light the quickened dead receive the anointing and refreshing grace. The soul saith to the quickened dead: "Look thou toward the east; for even as the east is the beginning of the sun's rise, so doth man come into birth eastward. Turn thy face westward if thou wouldst learn of death. And turn thy face eastward if thou wouldst learn of birth."

The larger congregation in the after-death state are those who have been slow to respond to their souls during life, but have had no evil vigor in their errors and mistakes. When the remorseful unrisen dead have concluded their purgatorial experience, they become the quickened dead. Their acceptance of the purgatorial instruction, while not exempting them from their future rectification in the coming life, frees them from the guilt feelings associated with their wrong works of former lives. In the next life, they enter the world accepting their disciplines, and their conscience guides them to avoid making the same mistakes once again. Those who have not responded to the instruction in the purgatorial caverns are born to the world in the next life with guilt in their hearts and minds, and with built-in resentments as to persons and conditions.

The quickened dead and the risen dead are aware of the ending of the after-death experience, and of the beginning of the birth-to-be. The unrisen dead who have failed to be remorseful in the purgatorial caverns are drawn into a womblike sleep previous to birth. Therefore, they are unaware of the transition between purgatory and the coming birth.

The quickened dead are in the Pavilions of Light, which are located or situated in close proximity to the First Heaven. The quickened dead behold the reflections of heaven, and intuit the heavenly presences nigh them. They are aware of the angels and the musics of heaven, but they do not experience them in the same manner as the risen dead. The risen dead are within the light; the quickened dead behold the light.

In the Pavilions of Light, there is neither sorrowing nor grieving; the quickened dead experience a joy reflected from the higher heavenly states. Many of the mystical reports of heaven relate to the Pavilions of Light. The golden streets, the gates of heaven, the angelic presences, the music—all of these relate to the Pavilions of Light.

When one who lives in the physical world has spiritual penetration to a Pavilion of Light in his dreams or during sleep, he moves among the inhabitants of the Pavilion of Light. He takes upon himself the joy of this lighted place. He is aware of a state of harmony, of peace—and more, of an anticipation; for the quickened dead in the Pavilions of Light are preparing to return to the world, and their uppermost feeling is a joyful anticipation of birth.

When one is in the throes of dying, he sometimes sees the faces of the quickened dead,
who are preparing to return to the world.
Also, when one meditates, he may see the
faces of those who prepare for birth. A person
living in the world, who has the power of
night-flight, frequently contacts the quickened
dead in his dreams.

The emotions and thoughts of the quickened dead, who are being prepared for birth,
are filled with the delight of basking within
the light showered upon them from heaven.
The reading of their souls' records of past
lives (revealing to them the justice of God's
equation), the light of heaven which is reflected downward upon their everlasting
bodies, and the instruction received in the
Halls of Learning—all prepare the quickened
dead to return to physical birth.

From time to time, the quickened dead are
taken by their Recording Angels to the reflected Archives of Life, Death, and Birth.
Here they are shown why there is a physical
existence, why men must die, and why repeated lives are necessary.

The time spent in the Pavilions of Light
may be likened to the earlier years of one's
physical life. It is a period of naïvete and
wonder—a period devoid of doubt and skepti-
cism. As the previous purgatorial state was
one of draining off or cleansing, the experience in the Pavilion of Light is one of total
receptivity.

When the quickened dead are ready for
birth, their Guardian Angels and Recording
Angels lead them to the blue pool of birth, or
pre-birth matrix. Even as the subtle-gravity
has the power to draw men into the caverns
of purgatory after death, there is a birth-
gravity or pull which reaches forth and draws
into the pre-birth matrix the earthbound, the
unrisen dead, the quickened dead and, in some
instances, the risen dead during the greater
tidal waves of reincarnation in the world.

When there are great reincarnation tidal
waves, the unremorseful unrisen dead are
caught up into the pre-birth matrix. Even
though some have not responded to the progressive states in the life after death, it is the
mercy of God that they be enabled to return

to the earth to rectify their former mistakes.

The unremorseful unrisen dead sleep during their entire time in the blue pool of birth; they experience the pre-birth matrix as an interior thunder upon their subconscious minds. If the forthcoming life is to be one of harsh discipline, they withdraw more deeply into the anesthesia-state.

The quickened dead are aware of the pre-birth matrix or blue pool of birth, and of their Guardian Angels and Recording Angels. They are aware of the coming life; the path of the future life is laid before them. Their future talents and creative potentials play upon their feelings and thoughts.

A very special work goes on between the Guardian Angels and the quickened dead previous to birth. The Guardian Angel enables one to be born to the world with acceptance. The Guardian Angel imprints upon the conscience level of the soul's record all that has occurred in the various caverns of purgatory, and seals in the grace of the instruction received in the Halls of Learning within the Pavilions of Light.

The Propagation Angels shepherd the quickened dead into the world through generation cyclic-tides of reincarnation. Many persons, who have not the will or the desire to be born again, return to the earth through the help of a reincarnation tidal wave. During a reincarnation tidal wave, masses of humanity are born to the earth, causing a population expansion and explosion. The unremorseful unrisen dead, who have slept for ages, are caught up into reincarnation tidal waves.

Men who have a genius for evil cannot reincarnate at will. They must await the greater reincarnation tidal waves to bring them to the earth. Those who understand the spiritual sciences may observe that when a civilization has reached its peak of ripeness, a nucleus of calloused, cruel and evil persons is born to the world, and the civilization begins its fall. This is the reason why, in the greater civilizations, there are ruthless rulers noted for their destructive works. Such men are known as *pawns of destiny*. Their malevolent ideas and deeds are an antidote to the crystallized evils in society. It is known by all sages that evil must destroy evil. As long as men have the slightest evil intent in their hearts, they will invite oppression from dominant and ruthless authorities. These violent episodes in history come that men may prepare for works of good.

When a man has minor errors and faults, and is less intent upon abusing his fellow man, he reincarnates more frequently. His lives are usually spaced hundreds of years apart, or, sometimes, even less. His inertias and errors are corrected through the competitive challenges in the world.

The risen dead are exempt from the cyclic reincarnation tides, as well as from the tidal waves of reincarnation; they are free to re-embody or return to the world at will. However, many of the risen dead choose to be born during a reincarnation tidal wave; for they find it necessary to contribute their knowledge and their gifts to the urgencies of the age or time.

While in the pre-birth matrix, the quickened dead and the risen dead may preview their future embryo development. In this, they learn that the soul is attached to the physical body when the embryo moves in the mother for the first time.

In the blue pool of birth, or pre-birth matrix, all who prepare for birth must unite themselves with the records of their former ancestral associations of other lives. This is called the *ancestral coordination.* Even as Jesus chose the line of David for His ancestry, and Mary and Joseph for His parents, so must all persons, with the exception of the unremorseful unrisen dead, come face to face with the ancestral coordination in the pre-birth matrix. The unremorseful unrisen dead sleep through the ancestral coordination in the pre-birth matrix. They are unaware of the ancestral line through which they are to be born, and they are unaware of the parents who will give them birth.

The quickened dead unite themselves with the future ancestral blood stream awaiting to give them birth, but they are unaware of the parents who will give them birth. The risen dead are aware of the ancestral line, and choose it for a specific purpose, so that the strength of their ancestral ties might supplement their works in the world. The risen dead are aware also of the parents who will give them birth. Long before birth, they are able to penetrate the mood and thoughts of their future parents.

Pure persons living in the world, who sincerely dedicate themselves as sacred channels for birth, invite the risen dead to be born through them. Even before conception, their souls and their inward selves are aware of the one seeking to come to the world. Their passionless yearning for a child reaches up and unites with the anticipatory joy of one desiring to bring the treasures of Spirit as sent from heaven.

If one sleeps through the ancestral coordination in the pre-birth matrix, he will express in his coming life either a fierce and possessive claim upon his ancestors and blood ties, or he will be devoid of respect and feeling for his parents and for other ties of blood. If one is aware of the ancestral coordination in the pre-birth matrix, and agrees with his soul to accept his ancestral virtues and flaws, he will be a responsible person in the family, and will be loyal to blood ties. If one is repelled by the ancestral record, he will enter the world resenting his ancestral ties; and, throughout life, he will blame his ancestry for his personal faults, deformities, or flaws.

The childhood of one who has been of the quickened dead is joyous, responsive, happy, and produces a love beyond defining in the lives of the parents. The childhood of one who has been of the unremorseful unrisen dead is unhappy, resentful, tempestuous, and brings uneasiness and anguish to those who give him birth. Those who give birth to the risen dead are touched by a sacred leaven which quickens the family atmosphere, and accelerates the evolvement to be gained through family and blood ties.

Men with Divine powers, such as the Elect and the greater prophets, are not required to return to the earth through re-embodiment or reincarnation. As a rule, they work from the heavenly kingdoms rather than in the physical world. Persons close to sainthood, and holy men who are lesser saviours, return to the world to bring a Divine message. They choose to take physical bodies during destructive times. It is their work to teach men of the heavenly ethic and wisdom, and to implant into receiving minds the seeds for spiritual beliefs.

8.

THE RISEN DEAD

The remnant of God, the handful of God, working for the holy cause, earning their seamless garments of worthiness, stand close to the Elect of heaven. The saintly prayers go forth from heaven, saying, "O save, protect and give succor to this blessed remnant. Let the praise of their works be sustained in heaven and in earth. And let this precious remnant dare to speak the words of the Spirit of Truth."

There is a rainbow canopy of etheric and luminous light encircling the earth. This canopy of pure light is called the First Heaven. The Saints, the true Prophets, the Holy Presences, the Elect, and the risen dead dwell in this habitation of pure light. The risen dead are a handful of God who dwell close to the Saintly Cloisters in the First Heaven. The First Heaven is the portal to the Kingdom of

138

God. All who dwell in the First Heaven are communicable to the higher and exalted states of heaven.

Those who have lived in the earth within the law of God, and have sought to extend His Word and His Way through their works, enter the state of death with freedom, lightness, joy. Their works of grace have enabled them to rise above the purgatorial caverns. Their hearts being contrite and tender, their trying sincere, and their ethic undeviated, they find themselves after death in the lighted corridors of the risen dead, where, in the splendor of great music, their vision of the true heaven is at last realized and confirmed. If the risen dead have known suffering or sorrows in their physical lives, these are assuaged in the holy atmosphere or vicinity of the Saints, wherein they are given comfort and solace, so that no remaining sorrow will cling to their minds or hearts.

The risen dead experience a holy anesthesia before awakening to heaven. This holy anesthesia enables the risen dead to adjust themselves to the light of heaven. The very power

of heaven's light upon one new to heaven induces a sleep—a sleep that gives joy to the
soul. The risen dead, so close to the presences
of heaven, are awakened one by one by their
Guardian Angels and Recording Angels.
After awakening from the holy anesthesia, the
risen dead are aware of the precincts or holy
communities of heaven. The risen dead find
themselves in the holy communities to which
they are adapted.

The Men in White Apparel come forth to
welcome and tutor those who find themselves
in the lighted corridors of the risen dead. The
Men in White Apparel prepare them for the
time when they shall begin their helps for the
new dead, and their greater or cosmic telepathic helps for the living. It is revealed to
the risen dead that, even as there is circumference, distance, and relativity in earth, in
heaven there are heavenly relativities. They
also are taught that each solar system or eternity has its own heaven, consisting of many
realms and kingdoms.

The various phases of instruction in the
lighted corridors of the risen dead are wafted

downward into the world of the living. Persons in the physical world who have spiritual and philosophical inclinations are influenced by this instruction in the daytime hours and sometimes in the dreams of the night.

When the risen dead have attained command of the magnification of their thought processes as expressed in heaven, they are taken to the Hall of Records, where they read the grace-records of their former lives and the grace-records of the lives of persons they have known intimately in the just previous life. The reading of the grace-records continues for a period of time, so that the risen dead, through extended logic, might incorporate into their minds the *Spirit-rationale*. This is a rationale beyond philosophy or retrospection. The Spirit-rationale stems from the Ultimates preordained from the beginning of the world.

After the reading of their records, the risen dead receive a holy insulation. Thereafter, it is impossible for the living to "bring up" or to willfully communicate with the risen dead. It is possible to "bring up" the unrisen dead;

it is also possible to intrude upon the quickened dead. However, no occult or psychic
power can touch or reach the insulated risen
dead.

RESPITE-INTERIMS

At regular intervals, the risen dead detach
themselves from the risen dead activity and
undergo a respite-interim, which is a form of
visual sleep. The closer one of the risen dead
comes to rebirth, the more frequently he falls
into a respite-interim. The risen dead must
undergo respite-interims previous to birth to
enable them to prepare for the coming life on
earth. In this, they do not review their past,
but they preview the coming life.

The unrisen dead undergo the respite-interims to modulate the harshness of the purgatorial experience. If one of the unrisen dead
has yet to die to his senses, he experiences in
the respite-interims a visible and audible pictorialization of beautiful environments. This
comes from the mercy of God, enabling even
the most bitter mind to behold beauty and
goodness, so that in the coming life he may

be prepared to respond more to the beautiful and the good.

In the lighted corridors, the risen dead use the soul-faculties rather than the senses. The risen dead respond to the visible and audible pictorialization in the respite-interims in a different manner than the unrisen dead. The risen dead experience sound and light as intelligence. Their emotions, free to function in the First Heaven, record the heavenly music as ecstatic love.

THE COSMIC SEASONS

During the four cosmic seasons, certain spiritual energies (angelic rain) fall upon men, giving vision and reassurance to their inner knowing and intuition. The four cosmic seasons are the winter solstice, the vernal equinox, the summer solstice, and the autumnal equinox. In each cosmic season, the Recording Angels, the Guardian Angels of the dead, and the Archangel* identified with the cosmic

*The Archangel Gabriel, winter solstice; the Archangel Raphael, vernal equinox; the Archangel Uriel, summer solstice; the Archangel Michael, autumnal equinox.

season literally pour down the angelic rain from heaven.

During the four cosmic seasons, the angels use the energies of the planets and the planetary fire centered within the jewels of the earth to transpose the heavenly telepathies to mankind. Man receives these telepathies upon his nervous system. His thoughts and emotions are sounding boards for the heavenly telepathies. Persons with immature emotions and thoughts receive the heavenly telepathies as a stirring of their consciences. Those who live reverently receive the cosmic telepathies as renewed purpose, vigor, joy.

In the cosmic seasons, the risen dead and the Recording Angels work closely with the living. The Recording Angels reveal certain cosmic truths to the spiritually inclined. The risen dead are fortified by the major spiritual impulses flowing into the earth; they are enabled in these periods to send their telepathies freely to the living. The risen dead send their assurances of the immortal life. Their heavenly love sent to their beloved ones in the world strengthens the living that they may bear their trials, and blesses them—giving them a super-courage to surmount and to overcome the rugged trials in the physical world.

The telepathies of the risen dead enter into the minds and hearts and affairs of the living in right timing. Some who live in the world intuit this knowledge and respond to it with awareness. Others who live in the world, being less certain of a life after death, interpret this help as a form of startling coincidence, or as some happy and special "good luck" for them. Regardless of the belief of the living, the risen dead come forth at intervals and give help to their loved ones, that their life on earth might be more hopeful, more blessed.

The heavenly, cosmic telepathies received by the living during each solstice and equinox are increased and magnified for approximately eighteen days. The cosmic telepathies enable the spiritual person to see the outer workings of his life as related to the inner plan. He may measure and weigh the events of his life with an eternal insight.

WINTER SOLSTICE

During the winter solstice, the Archangel Gabriel lifts the curtain on the birth panorama of the Lord Jesus. The living and the dead who revere life and hold it sacred undergo a spiritual birth to their souls. Those in the pre-birth matrix who joyously anticipate their coming birth receive a birth-blessing. The true drama of the birth of the Lord Jesus is revealed to them; in their coming lives, the star of Bethlehem will be understood, and the birth of the Lord Jesus will be more than a myth or a parable.

VERNAL EQUINOX

The Archangel Raphael accelerates the angelic activity during the spring or vernal equinox. The drama of the resurrection and of the ascension is experienced in heaven and in earth. Some of the earthbound dead are released from their states of confinement.

Many of the unrisen dead are drawn upward toward the quickened-dead state. The risen dead, rejoicing in the power of resurrection, go forth in a mighty company to welcome those who move upward toward the light in the world of the dead. The Archangel Raphael stirs the immortal image residing within the hearts of the living, and the Christ-Spirit quickens the spiritual potential in the minds of men.

SUMMER SOLSTICE

In the summer solstice, the Archangel Uriel, accompanied by the Guardian Angels and the Recording Angels, directs His light toward the pre-birth matrix. Men in the earth prepare to marry and to beget offspring. Families are reminded of their blood ties. Those who dwell in the unrisen-dead state enter into the reflected ancestral archives, where they read the reflected records of their former blood streams. They also learn of the river of life sustaining families and blood ties. The quickened dead who are ready for rebirth are taken to the pre-birth matrix in the summer solstice. Here they unite with the ancestral tie to come, and coordinate the ancestral history with their future-life habits and character. The risen dead enter into the ancestral archives of heaven and look upon the beginning of man's propagation compulsions in the world. They are instructed as to marriage and as to the true purpose of marriage.

AUTUMNAL EQUINOX

A special emphasis on repentance is placed upon both the living and the dead during the autumnal equinox. The living and the dead are offered the opportunity, through the Archangel Michael, to face their debts and to repent, or to atone. In the autumnal equinox the quickened dead, awaiting birth in the pre-birth matrix, read their former-life records. Their Guardian Angels give them the choice of three paths: (1) the path of family and blood tie discipline; (2) the path of struggle and self-attainment; or (3) the path of serving the human cause.

During the autumnal equinox, the risen

dead in the pre-birth matrix are enabled, through the Archangel Michael, to read the grace-records of the martyrs, the saints, and the prophets, and to take upon themselves the mantle of grace, so that they will not be led astray from their purpose in the world. There is but one path for the risen dead who are reborn to the physical world—the path of sacrifice and service. Even as Jeanne d'Arc, under the direction of the Archangel Michael, chose the harder way before coming to birth, so do all saints and martyrs enter the world without the expectation of a life of luxury and ease. When the risen dead live in the world, they choose simple and humble environments; for it is necessary that the spiritual person be free from materialistic hindrances and confinements.

> *But what went ye out for to see? A man clothed in soft raiment? behold, they that wear soft clothing are in kings' houses.*
>
> —St. Matthew 11:8

ILLUMINATI

One of the higher orders of the risen dead is that of the Illuminati. The Illuminati are creative titans. They are advanced men who lived in the world and produced mighty works of art, which taught men of the eternal realities and inspired them to live a spiritual life. After death, the Illuminati work with the Men in White Apparel to instruct the risen dead and the quickened dead who are destined to create in coming lives. The Illuminati also work with the living who are ripe to express their creative potentials. The greater art projects, such as immortal sculptures, music, murals, literature, and architectural structures are inspired by the telepathies of the Illuminati.

The Illuminati are in direct and frequent communication with the living. If one living has the knowledge of the Illuminati's over-direction and supervision, he learns that he receives his greater inspiration during certain times when the higher planetary energies are conducive to art, beauty, design, and perfect form; for the Illuminati use the higher degrees of light, extracted from the energies of the planets, to inspire those who would dedicate their genius to God.

LUNAR PROPAGATION ENERGIES

During certain negative phases of the moon, the earthbound dead and the unrisen dead, who have a strong ancestral retention, unconsciously use the lower lunar propagation energies to penetrate the emotions and thoughts of their descendents living in the world. This telepathic penetration exerts an inverted pressure upon the glandular system of the living. If one is unhappily married, this may cause a disturbance, and, sometimes, a disruption in the emotional and marital life. When the unmarried receive these earthbound or unrisen-dead glandular telepathies, they are likely to make hasty or wrong choice in marriage; for the compulsion to propagate will be greater than discrimination.

ORDINARY RECEPTION

When Jesus said, ". . . let the dead bury their dead" (St. Matthew 8:22), He was speaking of the risen dead who welcome or receive the new dead. The Men in White Apparel and the risen dead work in groups—

for the power of their combining magnifies their helps for the living and the dead. When the dead are ready to move beyond the bar of paradise into the deeper currents of purgatory, the Men in White Apparel and the risen dead may be seen two by two, sustaining and lifting those whose eyes are yet blinded by the brilliant light of paradise.

At the instant of death, some persons experience what is called the *ordinary reception*. Upon their first look into the world of heaven they see the beloved, remembered face of one loved by them and grieved for as dead in a former time. The Men in White Apparel assist the risen dead to come forth at the appointed time of the death of a loved relative or friend. When one has the grace to receive help from the Men in White Apparel and the risen dead, he has the feeling, immediately after death, that he is in a natural environment; and, thus, he enters the death state with naturalness and acceptance.

ANCESTRAL HEAVEN

The majority of people in the world believe

in an ancestral heaven where, after death, they will be reunited with their relatives, their families, and their ancestors. When persons are convinced that they will take up and continue in the same relationships after death with those who have died before them—be it husband, wife, father, mother, sister, brother, or child—this belief inhibits the after-death progression, and delays their upliftment in the afterlife. The angels, the Men in White Apparel, and the risen dead help such persons to understand that the life after death has five states: the withdrawn dead, the earthbound dead, the unrisen dead, the quickened dead, and the risen dead.

The secular belief that in death one will be reunited with his marriage mate or partner—and that they will live blissfully thereafter in heaven regardless of earth disagreements—prevents one from taking part in the after-death progressive rhythms, and he is in danger of becoming earthbound. The Men in White Apparel help such persons to accept the fact that, if the loved one is shut away in the caverns of purgatory, it is impossible after death for the one who has just died to be reconciled with his former mate. However, he may be given a brief overlook into the purgatorial cavern where the one he has loved is detained. In some instances, he may visit the cavern for a short interval and contact the one he seeks. The Men in White Apparel, the risen dead, and the angels of the one who has just died enable him to look into the cause, necessity, and justice related to the isolation of his beloved one.

If one who has died must undergo the purgatorial state, he is unable to be with those he loves who have achieved the risen dead state. When one with a pure heart dies, he spans the purgatorial abyss, and he is united with those whom he loves among the risen dead.

> *And Jesus answering said unto them, The children of this world marry, and are given in marriage:*
>
> *But they which shall be accounted worthy to obtain that world, and the resurrection from the dead, neither marry, nor are given in marriage.*
> —St. Luke 20:34,35

THE MOTHER-VEIL

Some of the risen dead in the lighted corridors work with the Mother-Veil of heaven.
The Mother-Veil risen dead work with the
Angels of Birth to remove from the dead the
fear of forthcoming birth, and they work with
the Angels of Death to remove from the living
the fear of impending death. During the
night's sleep, they also visit lonely and neglected children in the world.

A true mother in the world, being at all
times connected with the veil of life, receives
help from the Mother-Veil risen dead. The
veil of life sustains the love between the
mother and her children from birth to childhood and maturity. Mothers who abuse the
mother-child relationship are heavily laden
in the life after death. In the purgatorial experience of such mothers, the intensity of
their thwarted mother-love sometimes enters
into the dreams of children yet living in the
world. Their purgatorial experiences prepare
these women to pay their debt in coming lives
through some form of matriarchal sacrifice.

After death, sacred mothers are telepathically united with their children living in the world. When death comes, their influence upon their children is strengthened rather than lessened. It is possible for the sacred mother to work with the Guardian Angel of the child and to continually guide and direct the youthful years of the child. The Cherubim Angels work with such mothers to comfort their children in times of loneliness or neglect. A certain aroma of grace surrounds motherless children, enabling them to endure painful circumstances and environments.

All orphaned children have a close communion with their angels. If parents who have died have not the grace to help their children after death, the angels and the risen dead working with the Mother-Veil protect and shield these little ones.

The risen-dead father or mother is enabled, through the grace of God, to protect and overdwell the child, to comfort him, to stir his imagination, and to live in his world of dreams in the day and in the night. When a child is overdirected by a risen-dead parent, he is invariably the recipient of unusual helps from persons living in the world. The child may be adopted into a home where loving foster parents protect and guide him. Also, certain talents and gifts may be nurtured by the heavenly helps as sent from the parents.

THE RISEN DEAD AND THEIR BENEFIC TELEPATHIES

The risen dead use their benefic telepathies to heal and aid the sick. The risen dead work with the Guardian Angels of the living to warn them of danger and accidents; they sometimes send death-apprehension telepathies, preparing one for his demise or death. The risen dead also work to comfort the uneasy or anxious mind during sleep. When one living in the world is aware of night-flight, there are periods in which he works directly with the risen dead to give solace to those who grieve for the dead.

The risen dead work with the Saints to send holy fragrances to the living. These fragrances are inducted upon the fatigues of their loved ones. Sometimes, the living are consciously aware of these heavenly fragrances, or aromas of rejuvenation.

One of the ways the risen dead reach the thoughts of those they love is to send, through recollective telepathy, remembered musics associated with former memories. When the living inwardly hear a remembered, favorite strain of music, which sets up a recollective stream of ideas associated with the one who has died, this is a benefic telepathy from the risen dead, confirming their proximity and help.

When a statesman dies, he rests uneasily in the caverns of the unrisen dead if he has abused his power of authority and has compromised his country or nation. In purgatory, he works to recover his ethic, and to equalize his uneven works of the earth. The true statesman, who becomes one of the risen dead, is enabled to work with the archetype of his former nation, and, through benefic telepathies, to supervise and assist other dedicated statesmen within the nation.

When men are ready for a new religious impulse, a true prophet is born to the world.

When the prophet dies, he becomes one of the risen dead and continues his instruction through risen-dead telepathic powers. After death, he sustains an uninterrupted telepathy with those who followed his words. His telepathic overdwelling sustains the vitality of the religious ideas. The prophet overdwells the religious body until the beliefs are well established in the world, and until one in the company of his believers is ripe to inherit the mantle of leadership.

WEDDINGS BLESSED BY THE DEAD

When the quickened dead and the risen dead prepare to be reborn, they sometimes witness the marriage ritual of their parents-to-be. The angels of the one to be born, and the angels of those who are to give him birth, bless the wedding sacrament or ritual. It is often noted at such weddings that there has been an unusual reverence or feeling of love emanating from the environment. During the marriage ceremony, those in the audience who revere the marriage state receive a blessing as to their own marriage.

THE PURPOSE OF MAN

Many persons believe that they become angels after death. Men will never become angels. Man has a domain; the angels have a kingdom. The angelic kingdom has achieved its perfection; man has yet to reach his goal.

All animate and inanimate things of the earth are made up of particularizing atoms, identifying and classifying their intent and existence. The atoms of man and the atoms of angels are of different degrees of light. Man will never be an angel. He is a creature, a person, and a being. Through countless existences, the consciousness of man undergoes an unceasing transition and change. The purpose of man and his continuing flux in evolvement in this eternity system is that he produce a unique type of consciousness. Man is fortunate that he is accompanied by the angels, who shield him, protect him, and shepherd him in life and in death.

> *Thou madest him a little lower than the angels . . .*
>
> —Hebrews 2:7

True Saints, dwelling in the Cloisters of
the Saints in the First Heaven, do not re-
embody or reincarnate. Among the risen dead,
there are some close to sainthood who are
called the *worthy ones.* In crisis times, the
worthy ones choose to re-embody or to return
to the world. Certain worthy ones have been
titled "Saints" by men in the world. If there
be voluminous prayer-petitions going upward
to such worthy ones, these petitions cause the
worthy ones to be detained in the world of the
risen dead, thus delaying their return to the
earth.

A true prayer becomes an animate vehicle
in heaven. All pure prayers rise upward to
the Saintly Cloisters of heaven. True prayers
are received and differentiated in the seven
prayer cloisters of the Saints. If a prayer ful-
fills not the need of the soul, and pertains to
the selfish desires of a person, the prayer is
unable to rise beyond the darkened shadow
of one's soul's light. The answer or response
to the prayer must await the time when ethic
becomes equal to desire. If prayers are
founded upon faith, and are made with a

special covenant, these prayers go upward into
the garment or vicinity of the Lord Jesus.
Such prayers receive miraculous answers.

The risen dead are familiar with the power
and momentum of prayer. They behold the
prayers of men, the angelic helps accompanying prayers, and the differentiation of the varied degrees of prayers. The risen dead, when
sympathetic to some earth need, work with
the Saints in the transmutation of prayer. The
Saints transmute all pure prayers upward into
the garment of the Lord Jesus. Jesus and His
disciples dwell in the Third Heaven or Kingdom of God. All who pray to the Father in
the name of Jesus receive bountifully.

The risen dead, previous to rebirth, are instructed as to the Second Heaven where dwell
the Great Immortals, who are part of the
Elect. In this instruction, the risen dead learn
of the Planetary Angels, of the Host or Hierarchy. During this period, they incorporate
into their everlasting bodies the finer prisms
of spiritual light, which insulate them and
prepare them for future initiatory experiences
in the world.

For to this end Christ both died, and rose, and revived, that he might be Lord both of the dead and living.

—Romans 14:9

9.

GOD'S EQUATION

We weave today on the mighty loom of life and death. We sing our song, and move the shuttle vertical, horizontal—the cross of life. We follow the pattern cast after the myriad stars. We pause, and then again we weave. We think on Saturn's Day, and of our Loved Dead. We seal them in to life, love, light, to the going forth in memory of God to another day. We weave a pattern unto the Day of Rest.

Man is not on the earth for aimlessness. He lives to create. The Plan of God is infinite variety, so that man may become versatile, enlarged, creative. Each life is a pattern similar to that of other lives; yet, by necessity, each contains something different. He who despairs, thinking one life to be all, has not seen the Light.

The body of man is but a covering for the flame of the soul. Each one who enters the world has received his orders from his soul to journey forth, to discover, to experience, and to create. If he fails to remember the formula for life, he falls into pathetic states.

In the world of the dead, there is neither punishment nor condemnation; all are instructed with love. The theme of justice and mercy is never absent. When one has resisted what life has offered, his understanding after death is slow and unresponding. Words of instruction are repeated into the mind again and again until, with time, absorption occurs.

One of the greatest attributes God has given to man is the power to choose and to will. Even in the state of death, the will of the individual is intact. One may or may not choose to receive the help of the Men in White Apparel. The Men in White Apparel never withdraw their helps from the dead. Their instruction, though seemingly disregarded by the earthbound dead or the sleeping dead, is imprinted upon their emotions and thoughts.

In the physical world, there are reflexes of

the body; in the life after death, there are reflexes of the soul. After death, the pulsation
of the soul becomes the heartbeat of the everlasting body. The angels, the risen dead, and
the Men in White Apparel aid one who has
died to orient himself to the use of the everlasting body and to the environment in which
he is placed after death. If one believes in a
life after death, he has better command of his
everlasting body, and is at home in the after-
death world.

The power of the soul neither temporizes
nor compromises. During life and death, the
power of the soul works continually to modulate and to adjust. If a person has erred while
living in the physical world, and has an uncontrite heart after death, the power of the
soul must adjust the weighted darkness shad-
ing the conscience. Acts of cruelty and malice
are weighed after death upon the scales of the
soul. A cruel person finds it difficult to be
completely remorseful in the after-death interval. When a cruel person returns to the world,
he is given the opportunity to resolve something of the debts incurred in a life of deliber-

ate deviation from the soul's intent. Heavy debts incurred during one life in the physical world often require many lives of rectification and adjustment.

The record of one's wrongdoing is imprinted upon the outer fringe of the soul's medallion. This causes a discordant note, called the *vibratory hum*. When the vibratory hum of the soul's medallion is congested, one remains close to the earth after death and is earthbound, or of the unrisen dead. Upon the luminous area of the soul's medallion, there is imprinted the record of one's good works or grace. When there is more grace action than vibratory hum activity, the everlasting body is free to arise after death into the dimensions of heaven; in such instances, a person becomes one of the company of the risen dead.

The Word of God contains seven great creative tones. These tones work with the soul of man. When man is at one with his soul, he responds to the Word of God with a noble mind and a loving heart. The laws of God, and the disciplines stemming therefrom, are

the result of Saturn's tone falling into the
earth. In each life, man learns to command
something of the somber Saturn tone of pain
in the earth. This tone correlates to the note
of "Fa" on the keyboard of music. When man
willingly obeys the laws of God, he becomes
communicable to "our Father which art in
heaven." He who masters the Fa tone, or becomes at one with the Father, shall earn the
power of resurrection and shall no more know
the second death, but shall go in and out as
a true laborer in the vineyards of God.

> *To him that overcometh will I give to eat
> of the hidden manna, and will give him a white
> stone, and in the stone a new name written,
> which no man knoweth saving he that receiv-
> eth it.*
>
> —Revelation 2:17

Within God's equation, there are three
laws. These may be called the checks and
balances within the Eternal Will. They are
the Just Law, the Right Law, and the Good
Law. The Just Law imposes the discipline
caused by deviation in past lives and in the
present life. The Right Law teaches, de-

scribes, and interprets the Will of God. The Good Law times the grace to the one who observes and also does the Will of God.

Death comes under the Right Law. The Right Law works with the timing of the soul. Viewing of the debts of past lives is activated after death through the Right Law.

The Just Law teaches the one who has died how to accept the correction of wrong acts as being "just" for him. The Right Law discloses to him how he may overcome his debts. And the Good Law shows him the harmonious outcome for having fulfilled this triune action within the Will of God.

When one has earned righteousness through his earth works, he will return to the earth as a righteous man who takes upon himself the responsibility of assuming the burdens of those who are yet unable to understand the equation of God.

HOLY DEATH-ANESTHESIA

If a person in the dying state has lived a life of purity—and has earned grace through works of good—those who stand near and by him during the hours of dying are enabled to unite their prayers with the grace of the one dying. The Angels of Death then come forth and induce the holy death-anesthesia, and build a welcoming pathway of light for the one dying.

AFTER-DEATH WILL

There are some who die who, by lack of practicality, have failed to make financial provision for their loved ones who live. Such persons, after death, are unable to rest or to come to peace with themselves. If their love be great enough for the living, they are given the power to make an after-death will. Through telepathic power, they may send their thoughts to the living, showing them how they may use certain latent resources. The loving dead are given the grace to stand by and aid the living until the after-death will is consummated.

ANNIVERSARY OF DEATH

There is a resurgence of memory between the living and the dead which occurs each year on the day one has died. The annual solar-tide, working with the souls of men, affects the living and the dead. In the solar-tide, there is a brief period of uniting between the soul of the one dead and the soul of the one living. This is acutely felt when there has been a close bond of pure love, or when something is unresolved through deep hate. On the anniversary of death, the living may use the momentum of the solar-tide to give vitality to their prayers for the dead.

BIRTHDAY OF THE DEAD

When one who has passed on has failed to undergo the second death, and still lives in the previous-life memories, there will occur on the birthdate of the just former life a strong telepathic compulsion between the one dead and those living who are related to him by blood. This will be experienced within the thoughts, and sometimes within the dreams of the living. On this significant birthday anniversary, the shadow of regret for the wasted years of the previous life (of the unrisen dead) has the power to penetrate and depress the thoughts of the living.

Those who have become the quickened dead, or the risen dead, and those who have been sainted in heaven have the power to send a very special telepathic blessing to the world on the birthday anniversaries of their just previous life.

10.

THE CARE OF THE DEAD

*Who is competent to speak of death? Only
that one who has remembrance of the experiences between death and birth is competent to
speak of death. Only that one who has the Saturn
power of Ritual, given to him in the beginning
of this eternity, can give solace to those who
grieve for the dead. He who has the grace to
receive the Saturn Ritual at death has the power
to die with naturalness; he releases himself to
the Angels of Death with peace. He who has not
the grace to receive the true Death Ritual must
look into the faces of the Purgatorial Angels.
The Angels of Purgatory have many faces. If
one is sorrowful, the Angels of Purgatory have
faces of sorrow. If one has conscience, the
Angels of Purgatory have faces of conscience.*

Those who have little understanding of the
soul, and of the timing of the soul, sometimes

offend the ethic in the care of the dying. When the Angel of Death stands ready to draw the one dying over the threshold of death, and the living seek to interfere with the timing of death, this is an offense to the dying. Primitive peoples of the world have retained certain knowledge as to the care of the dying and of the dead. The more cultured the people, the less understanding there is as to the care of the dying and of the dead.

In the scientific age, men are in danger of offending the death ethic. As painful and incurable diseases appear in the world, men with scientific skills are sometimes tempted to apply their skills to render euthanasia or mercy death. When a person precipitates the death of another by his own hand, the commandment, "Thou shalt not kill," is offended. Also, when any human agent seeks to extend life beyond the time limit as ordained by the soul, dying persons become the victims of blind mercy. When life is extended beyond the timing of the soul, the one dying is subjected to a painful purgatorial experience, while yet in the body.

Men are close to many new discoveries which will benefit them through science. However, no human person, regardless of skills or anatomical knowledge, can with true ethic tamper with the laws of God. Those who interfere with the intent of the soul in death or life open the door to tragic lessons for themselves.

All who serve the weak and minister to the dying and the dead will gradually come to understand the ethics in the care of the sick and of the dead. At the latter part of the scientific age, a mighty mercy impulse will come to the world. The working of the soul will be less of a mystery and will be better understood. The care of the sick and the dead will be expressed more sacredly, more reverently.

Embalming or preserving of the physical body after death is an ancient art. The original purpose of embalming was to keep the one dead close to the environment of his physical life, and to detain him from reincarnating.

It is grace when a person is not embalmed. Coordination between death and the life after death is a necessity to the one who dies. If this coordination is disturbed—by embalming, by premature cremation, or by premature burial —there is distress and confusion in the thoughts, and one suffers disorientation in the world of the dead.

Rest and quiet are essential in the three days after the expiration of the breath from the physical body. If a person is embalmed during the three-day after-death repose, this distracts the one dead and interferes with his after-death retrospection. An embalmed person also finds it more difficult to assemble his soul-faculties after death.

There is slowly entering the world a sacred care of the dead. The living are inspired to aid their loved dead by having the body placed in a cool place for the period of three and one-half days* after death. After the three and one-half days, the physical body is then placed into the flames and cremated.

In the present age, more and more persons having spiritual knowledge are aware of the importance of the retrospection during the

* The modern Ritual for the Dead adds twelve hours to the three-day period as a precautionary measure against intrusion upon the dead.

first three days after death. Such persons instruct their loved ones to place their bodies in refrigeration after death—without embalming; for they know that the withdrawal of the blood from the body in these three important days prevents them from having a peaceful death retrospection. Persons who are highly evolved know that the blood is not only a life essence, but that it also has the power to photograph and record the emotions and the thoughts of man. For three days after death, the blood of man is living blood, and contains the animation and vitality of the life just lived. When the body is not embalmed, one is more directly communicable to the pictured emotions and thoughts imprinted upon the blood. When one is embalmed, his Guardian Angel must transpose the pictures to his feelings and thoughts, and he experiences them in an indirect, rather than in a direct manner.

As men grow more land-hungry, embalmment and preservation of the physical body after death will cease. There will no longer be cemeteries or crypts. Cemeteries will be replaced by community memorials containing

the names of the dead. A death enrollment
or record will be inscribed in bronze upon
the walls of the public memorial. Fifty years
after the death, the name of the person will
be removed. Only in the rare instance of great-
ness will the name be preserved. These memorials will be supported by the governments,
and will be kept in small garden-like spaces
reverently preserved. They will become sacred
shrines in their communities.

When men move out of the crude phase of
the scientific age, harmless X-ray techniques
will be used to observe the living functions of
the human body. These techniques will make
obsolete the dissection of the dead and autopsy
after death. Embalming, burial, and cremation will become outmoded customs. Certain
ultrasonic and electronic energies will be used
to disintegrate the body after death.

THE DEATH RITUAL

In the present age, there are differences of
opinion as to the care of the body after death.
The ritual observed by the living for the dead
should correlate to the sacraments of heaven;

for all true rituals and sacraments originate in heaven. Those who conduct the death ritual, and are uncertain as to the reality of a life after death, fail in their help for the dead. A true ritual should give comfort to the living, and peace to the dead. Until those who minister to the dead are initiated into the true ritual for the dead, the angels must stand by to give succor to the dead and strength to the living.

Regardless of what words are said during the moments of a death ritual, each man writes his own eulogy with his life works. However, when words are said which correlate to the true eulogy of the life, this empowers the one who died to rise.

The greatest eulogy to give peace to the dead is music. Music accompanying the death ritual should be of an impersonal nature, disassociated from sentimental attachment. Music, flowers, and lighted candles enable the angels to come closer to the dead and to those who grieve for the dead. Music makes it possible for the angels to magnify the drama of the death experience for the one who has died; music also aids in the transition and rise in death. Through the help of the angels, one may come close to his Recording Angel and read his judgment scroll with less apprehension and fear.

The living should be careful to observe to the letter the form of death ritual one has requested or believed-in previous to death. Enforcing an unfamiliar ritual upon the dead is a breach of a spiritual ethic.

When there is doubt as to what death ritual should be used, the Lord's Prayer, the Twenty-third Psalm, a few passages of the words of Jesus, and the death ritual as given by Solomon in Ecclesiastes (Chapter 12, verses 1 through 7) may be read or spoken reverently.

In the First Heaven—where dwell the Saints, the Men in White Apparel and the risen dead—the names of those about to die and the names of all who have recently died are called each Saturday morning, at the time corresponding to 11 a.m. in each area on earth. One may best pray for the dead on Saturday morning at 11 a.m. To pray for the new dead on the Saturday following the death assists in the rise and upliftment of the one dead. When one prays for the dead at 11 a.m. on Saturday morning, he works with the rhythm of the souls of the dead; his prayers unite with the heavenly helps for the dead.

If one continually dreams of a person who has died, he should pray for the one dead for a period of three days after the dream. Such prayers will fortify the one dead to arise above an earthbound state.

Prayers by the living for the dead enable the angels to come closer to the dead. The earthbound dead and the unrisen dead, unaware of their angels, are made more aware of the angels by the prayers of the living.

EARTHQUAKES AND THE DEAD

Whenever earthquakes occur in the earth, the sleeping dead are briefly awakened; the unrisen dead become more aware of their angels; and, in the area where the earthquake is active, the earthbound dead are dislodged from their static environments. When the inner strata of the earth are disturbed by earthquakes, the earthbound dead have the opportunity to be free of their obsessions, and to become part of the company of the unrisen dead. Some of the quickened dead prepare to be born in the environment where the earthquake occurred. The subconscious minds of men living within the environment of the earthquake are stirred, and the consciences of men become more sensitive.

During the time of the resurrection of Jesus, a mighty earthquake occurred, etherically affecting the complete earth and the purgatorial caverns. This terrestrial shaking pressed upon the heart-atoms of mankind. Since the time of Jesus' resurrection, the consciences of men, in death and in life, have had a greater reproving action.

> *Jesus, when he had cried again with a loud voice, yielded up the ghost. And, behold, the veil of the temple was rent in twain from the top to the bottom; and the earth did quake, and the rocks rent; And the graves were opened; and many bodies of the saints which slept arose, And came out of the graves after his resurrection, and went into the holy city, and appeared unto many. Now when the centurion, and they*

that were with him, watching Jesus, saw the
earthquake, and those things that were done,
they feared greatly, saying, Truly this was the
Son of God.

—St. Matthew 27:50-54

THE RESURRECTION

As the senses in the physical life go outward
to explore, in death the senses turn inward
and explore the inner man, his motives, his
purpose, and his placement in the plan of life.

During the physical life, men are fascinated
by the seasons and the elements; they have an
innate compulsion and desire to master the
elements. In this age, they create and design
machines, boats, craft, so that they might skim
upon the waves, fly in the air, and master the
confinement of gravity and the limitation of
space. When death comes, man must acclimate
himself to a life beyond gravity. He must
accustom himself to the everlasting body, to
its range and circumference. He must re-estab-
lish within himself a vision of greater magni-
tude, and that which has been formerly his
sense perception must be replaced by a form

of thought and feeling beyond that used in the gravity world.

When man loses by death one he loves, and has full understanding of death and the body everlasting, he overcomes something of his own death experience. After death, he will know the helps of angelic mediation, and he will have a greater range of action for his everlasting body.

When men live in the physical world, they are encased in four bodies. These bodies are the physical body, the etheric body, the emotional body, and the mental body. At death the physical body of man disintegrates; its essential atoms and chemistry go back into the cradle of nature. The etheric body has two parts: a lesser etheric body and a higher etheric body. When one dies, the lesser etheric body becomes a fire, enabling the physical body to be destroyed. The higher etheric body becomes the everlasting body after death.

The emotional body also has two parts. At the moment of death, the lesser emotional body, which correlates to the purgatorial world, begins a dissolution. This is called the

second death. When the one who has died has
released himself from the lesser emotional
body through the varied stages of purgatory,
he is free to function in his higher emotional
body, his mental body, and his higher etheric
body. The higher etheric body is the everlasting or spiritual body.

> . . . *There is a natural body, and there is a*
> *spiritual body.*
> —1 Corinthians 15:44

> *But some man will say, How are the dead*
> *raised up? and with what body do they come?*
> —1 Corinthians 15:35

Jesus, being a priest after the order of
Melchisedec, used the power to manifest and
to de-manifest. Therefore, in the three-day,
after-death interim, Jesus self-cremated His
physical body. He de-manifested His physical
body, His lesser etheric body, and His lesser
emotional body through spiritual power.

> *Jesus answered and said unto them, Destroy*
> *this temple, and in three days I will raise it up.*
> *Then said the Jews, Forty and six years was this*
> *temple in building, and wilt thou rear it up in*
> *three days? But he spake of the temple of his*

*body. When therefore he was risen from the
dead, his disciples remembered that he had said
this unto them; and they believed the scripture,
and the word which Jesus had said.*

—St. John 2:19-22

*For as Jonas was three days and three nights
in the whale's belly; so shall the Son of man be
three days and three nights in the heart of the
earth.*

—St. Matthew 12:40

After His resurrection, Jesus manifested Himself to Mary Magdalene in the garden. She failed to recognize Him, because His higher etheric body was unfamiliar to her. Jesus commanded her "Touch me not," for He had yet to assemble His higher etheric body and to coordinate it with the after-death state.

*Jesus saith unto her, Touch me not; for I am
not yet ascended to my Father: but go to my
brethren, and say unto them, I ascend unto my
Father, and your Father; and to my God, and
your God.*

—St. John 20:17

Jesus, being the Messiah, was able to linger close to His disciples for forty days after death to teach them and to instruct them as to their future apostleship. During this period, Jesus went in and out of the purgatorial worlds, for it was His last mission to free the earthbound dead who had lingered in purgatory for aeons of time.

> *(Now that he ascended, what is it but that he also descend first into the lower parts of the earth? He that descended is the same also that ascended up far above all heavens, that he might fill all things.)*
>
> —Ephesians 4:9,10

When the forty days after His death had concluded, Jesus "ascended up far above all heavens," where He now dwells, and is the Lord over the living and the dead.

Jesus is the perfect blueprint or prototype for man. When Jesus ascended into the Third Heaven, both the living and the dead, in some degree, were lifted up. As the ages unroll, those who believe in Him, and know Him to be the Son of Man, will become "like him." When men become like Jesus, there will be no dying or death.

And I, if I be lifted up from the earth, will draw all men unto me.

—St. John 12:32

Beloved, now are we the sons of God, and it doth not yet appear what we shall be: but we know that, when he shall appear, we shall be like him; for we shall see him as he is. And every man that hath this hope in him purifieth himself, even as he is pure.

—1 John 3:2,3

And God shall wipe away all tears from their eyes; and there shall be no more death, neither sorrow, nor crying, neither shall there be any more pain: for the former things are passed away.

—Revelation 21:4

INDEX

A

adolescent 54

adulterer 77

adultery 78

afterlife 4,40,42,45,70,71,73,85,98,153

agnostic 2

alcohol 80

alcoholics 80

amoral 55,56

ancestral 22,34,134,135,147,148,151-153

anesthesia, death 6

       holy 139,140

       pre-birth 100

       purgatorial 85

       tides of 100

angelic choirs 30

angelic host 59

Angel of Death 5,173

angels 10,15,29,30,49,54,57,59,85,101,128,144,153,154,
    156,159,160,162,166,179,181,184

Angels of Birth 155

Angels of Death 10,16,25,155,170,173

Angels of Purgatory 173

animal 110,123,124

Antichrist 102

apparitional body 101

apparitional dead 101,102

Archangel Gabriel 143,146

Archangel Michael 143,148,149

Archangel Raphael 143,146,147

Archangel Uriel 143,147

archetypal cord 30-32

archetypal hum 32

architecture 150

cynical mind 11
cynicism 9,12

D

death-anesthesia, holy 169,170
Death Angel 21,22
Death Angels 20
Death Ritual 173,178-181
death wish 7
disciples 16,110,162,186
dreamlike sleep 39,40
dreams 21,54,65,72,89,115,128,129,141,155,156,171,181

E

ear 29
ear, inner 28
earthbound 8,67,80,90,98,99,106-109,111-114,118-121,
    123,130,165,167,181
earthbound dead 54,64,75,79,80,93,98-103,105,106,
    109-113,146,151,153,181,187
earthquakes 6,181,182
Easter 89
East Indians 114
ego 106
egotist 58
Egypt 119,120
Elect 16,43,61,65,66,136,138,162
elementals 119,120
embalming 175-178
embryo 31,134
emotional body 67,80,101,184,185
emotions 19,36,54,56,64,66-68,77,81,99,102,121,123,129,
    143,144,151,165,177
entities 79,80,105,106,108,109,113-115,118
entity 80,102,105-109,117-119
eternal laws 61
eternal life 12,30,41,69

193

grace-blessing 61
grace, touch of 14,61
grandparents 21
gravity-bound dead 121-123
Great Immortals 162
grief 8-12,15,18,19,30,48
Guardian Angel 4,5,21,30,56,96,131,156,177
Guardian Angels 15,130,131,140,143,147,148,157

H

Hall of Records 141
Halls of Learning 129,131
hallucinatory caverns 80
hate 11,49,52,60,84,91,171
head, crown of 31,37
healing 29,54,57
heart 9,23,24,27,30-32,36,37,39,45,47,51,56,68,72,74,
    78,84,93,94,115,154,166
hearts 38,62,66,92,102,133,139,145,147
heaven 2-4,9,15,19,27,30,37,40,42,57,59-61,68,71,76,89,
    90,95,98,104,121,122,127-129,135,136,138-141,146,
    148,152,153,155,167,172,178
heaven, ancestral 152,153
heavenly presences 57,128
hell 4,24,63
Hierarchy 162
higher worlds 23,30,42,46,89
Holy Ghost 8
Holy Presences 138
humor 22
hypnosis 106,109
hypocrisy 72,73
hypocrite 72,73

I

illness 7,18-20
Illuminati 59,149,150

197

S

throat 31,32,37
tobacco 80
tone 29,30,35
transmigration 110
truth 45,55,97

U

umbilical cord 30
underworld, subtle 68-71,102,105
unrisen dead 64,65,67,76,88,98,125,126,130-132,
    134,136,141-143,147,151,153,167,171,172,181,182

V

vernal equinox 143-146
violence 4-6,55,60,100

W

war 4,6
weary dead 88
weddings 159
well-meaning dead 99
Western world 114
will 24,34,36,56,66,100,105-107,114,117,118,132,165
Will of God 5,13,26,57,169
winter solstice 143,144-146
wisdom 22,30,137
witch of En-dor 103,104
withdrawn dead 86,153
works 2-4,24,41-43,46,50,61,72,138,139,158,167,169
world-subconscious 63
worship 90,102
worthy ones 161
writers 60

Y

yoga 114